THE LAST GERALDINE OFFICER

By Thomas McCarthy

Poetry

Fiction

Memoir

THOMAS McCARTHY

The Last
Geraldine
Officer

ANVIL PRESS POETRY

Published in 2009
by Anvil Press Poetry Ltd
Neptune House 70 Royal Hill London SE10 8RF

Copyright © Thomas McCarthy 2009

ISBN 978 0 85646 421 8

This book is published
with financial assistance from
Arts Council England

A catalogue record for this book
is available from the British Library

Designed and set in Monotype Ehrhardt by Anvil
Printed and bound in Great Britain
by Hobbs the Printers Ltd

for
Theo Dorgan, Joe Gavin
and Patrick Cotter

Acknowledgements

To the editors of the following publications where many of
the poems were first published:

*Agenda, Cork Literary Review, Cyphers, The Irish Times,
Poetry Ireland Review, Poetry Review, Qualm, RTE* Radio
One, *Southword, The Stinging Fly, Times Literary Supplement,
The Ulster Tatler.*

The author gratefully acknowledges the assistance of Séamus
Ó Rodaigh, scholar and teacher, in editing the 1940s Irish
poems of Colonel FitzGerald of Templemaurice House.

Contents

Part One

The Fiction, The Sea

Part Two

Part One

The Fiction, The Sea

Moonlight Cooler, 1948

It was the four frosted tiki-stem cocktail glasses,
Survivors of a disreputable Irish bar in Minneapolis,
That you were most proud of on the day
Of the Ballysaggart races; that day when a man
Claiming to be Bing Crosby, or Bing's brother,
Walked into the pub with a Fine Gael Senator.
Both wore dinner jackets. The Senator's hunter
Had been lamed, hence the intense celebration
To mask his personal sadness. Two women,
Elegant and loud, followed them indoors:
Mrs. Norah Foley said they were like goddesses,
The way they could move without moving, so to speak –
She watched them with the eyes of a wet
Sheep-dog as she threw lumps of turf on the fire.
You were non-plussed when they mentioned
The word 'cocktail', thinking to embarrass us all
In the parishes of Ballysaggart and Lismore.
Sure every baptized Christian in the county knew,
In them days, that on a moonlit evening in November
Two ladies on the way to dinner at a Big House
Would have the juice of one lemon, a little sugar,
Two Irish ounces of Calvados, and soda; all
Shaken with a bit of ice from O'Connor's fish store
And strained into – pardon the lack of highballs –
Your tiki-stem cocktail glasses fit for any Bing.

Molly Keane's Peach Champagne

It was a most ordinary Irish evening at the end of
A windy day; leaves scattering with a nonchalance
Learned early in the autumn of their lives,
When the phone rang with the raspiest grumble
Our old phone always had, the black one
That blocked the small ships in Denis's little
Maritime oil sketch by Mr. Atkinson of Cork;
Grumbling away until I picked it up, heavy as
A cine-camera that the postman used to have
To record the Corpus Christi processions –
I mean the processions before Ireland went to
The dogs – the postman who once delivered
A white wrought-iron bench from Fred Astaire;
And picking up the phone I heard *herself*, Molly,
Just out of hospital after a near fatal heart attack,
Just out of hospital and straight back to work:
'Writing is so wearisome,' she says, 'I find that
Lobster and peach champagne do keep one going.'

An Old Fashioned, 2006

for Maurice Hayes

I was sitting there in the old Shelbourne Bar
With my daughter, Kate Inez,
Drinking the most flagrant if not fragrant
Cocktail in the whole universe,

When a man walked in and offered me
A distributor's licence for *Waterford* glass.
Be careful what you long for, my daughter said:
She is wise like her mother. But my dreams

Seemed to come true at that moment;
And the greatest dream of all, to handle
Only the finest crystal: I would go to the end
Of my days handling only the Lismore suite.

As the ice melted in the Bourbon glass
I thought of all the idiots Prince Myshkin met
In Dostoevsky's books; disillusioned
Soldiers, drunk and despondent husbands,

The truly demented at each border station. I thought:
I've made poems for all of them, for years.
Why shouldn't I celebrate a great craft now –
For old Mr. Penrose, for the ages? For pure crystal.

On Becoming a Person

And you were just saying yourself, *yoosir*, you were saying
How this country has gone to the dogs. Gone entirely.
Just now as you settled adroitly inside Paax Foley's Pub,
Having been nearly run over by a young pup in an SUV,
A black yoke with the sinister wheels of a combine-harvester;
As you were very nearly shredded to binder-twine,
You remarked how manners had gone the way of the Latin Mass.
God be good to those who spoke words we couldn't understand;
They were a blessing and consolation. They were a safety-pin
That kept the wet trousers of Ireland from falling down.
Speaking of dogs, I said. Did you notice a strange thing
About Mrs. Norah Foley's collie? It may be a sign of our times,
But the old dog has been chewing, chapter by chapter,
The last library copy of Carl Rogers' *On Becoming a Person*.

Early Evening at Ballyferriter

Wild screams from two Irish Language classes
As they enter the cold sea, a sea now
Of unsteady adolescent colours, a great chorus
Of disturbed sea-water: one brave

Boy-grammarian splashes the others
And dives into the protective deep.
I turn and fix my gaze on the far shore,
Waiting, like the patient violinist

Giuliano Carmignola, in Locatelli's
Concerto No. 10 for violin, strings and continuo,
Waiting for the returning wave of salt
That crashes orchestral upon the swimmers,

But see, instead, the conductor's flash
Of a gannet as it wheels and dives with metallic fire:
Boy, bayonet and baton, splitting open
The vast summer we share, and its arrangement.

Conversazione, with Sea and Man

A middle-aged man with a hurling-stick
Plays frantically with the early August waves,
And I have this fanciful idea:
He is a performance artist on a Government grant;

This is a Cuchulain performance,
Wet and heroic, captured by his red-haired child
With a digital camera; and somewhere in Dublin
A cutting-edge curator is waiting by her screen;

Or what I see is a sand-portrait of my own life,
Art calling me to account for myself,
Questions from this life winnowed on the Kerry surf
With all the urgency of something being flailed in the sea.

But wait: I walk in the direction of the beaten waves
And find, instead, a stinging Portuguese man-o'-war,
Its head like a crown of thorns
As it dissolves inexorably into grains of sand.

Broken Promises

As we grow older we become adept collectors
Of broken promises. It's not that the world means ill,
But the world's options grow larger
Day by day. Too much hanging around
By the likes of ourselves; and too much excitement,
Far too much excitement, by a world
That rushes headlong to embrace new recruits.

The young are beautiful and sanguine.
That's for sure. As I was saying,
I hate that you promised me so long ago
An exceptional copy of Ptolemy's *Geographica*,
The one published by Hol of Ulm
With its elaborately coloured vellum maps:
That gift to you from Prince Eugene of Savoy –

As for the 1480 book printed by Lettou of London,
I'll let it pass. People forget, and I
Work all day in a faraway library. But my heart
Did leap when you left the Penguin *Selected*
Of Yevtushenko. It smelled of camp fires
And young Georgian wines: I've had it
Bound in vellum, like an original Jensen of Venice,

And I take it with me on long journeys,
To the Kerry mountains, to Shanghai, to the sea.
Once, while reading it,
A young woman approached me, wearing Stuart plaid,
Claiming that her name was Larissa Fyodorovna,
That the book was of her patrimony –
I promised her the book, of course, before I fled.

The Fiction, The Sea

for Catherine

You keep returning to the sea as if you'd lost a bracelet
In the water, or some such valuable and peaceful thing.
It is part of the problem of being a girl, my mother
Always said, such possessions as become windows
And mirrors to call a woman back, to demand closing –
Or as Henry James said, for he was no mother,
As the picture is reality so the novel is history
And not as the poem is: a metaphor and closed thing.
Strange how I could never go back to that spit of sand,
The sea-warren of the Cunnigar, in Dungarvan Bay,
For I would never want to deconstruct what was
Never whole, what was tentative and poorly given;
What it was that I chased after among blue razor shells.
But I digress, for this is about you, returning late
In the summer to a wild and restless sea; it is you
Grown restless from inadequate sunshine, turning back
Like a pilgrim to inhale the iodine of the far West;
Going farther, as you must, to meet the sea half-way,
The sea in its life being more entrenched than us
And far more Flaubertian. So what of your bracelet,
Then, and where did that come from? Nothing but salt
At the very edge of summer before it flips away forever,
Salt and sand that makes a kind of mirror, nothing but salt
Is left on the hard pavement out of the sea and kelp too,
And its iodine; all strewn on the cold water. As you figure
And pick among things like a novelist, the tide bathes
Your whitened toes, it advances and recedes. My own
Beloved, the sea's droll pathos kisses you: it is your fable-
Spinner, giving us knowledge abundant and vicarious.

Well, Look at You

I *Correspondents*

We make love again after a long journey
Through the Sunday newspapers.
Our bed shakes with the crackle of news –
Observer, *Tribune*, *Indo* and *Business Post*.

How far apart we were
While gathering such news.
Our stories for each other went astray
Like colour supplements.

You've always been my favourite reading –
A columnist who covered all our love-life,
Mary Welch Hemingway of the heart.
See how copy-editing you makes me lyrical,

Changing all Contents to listen to your report:
Not the knowledge but the colour,
Not the bare facts but the facts bare. And this:
Fade to advertisement, your voyager's kiss.

II *Your Ordinary Gesture*

By the time I reach the kitchen full of the most ordinary
        longing,
Thinking how we might extract ourselves from this life,
How we might find a place together in an unfashionable county,
Like O . . . . . y, for example, or maybe the southern part of
        C . . . . w –

Somewhere less complex than a busy city – where the new pups
And the three cats can wander freely. At this stage, if I could have
You and you only I'd go on the roads. No question about it.
Come with me, girl. During the war I dreamt only of the two
    of us.

Thinking thus, I smelled your *Dunn Bros* coffee brewing
And I caught you, before you became self-conscious, unself-
consciously polishing your black shoes, dressed formally
For work. Let me tell you how that was, how perfect you looked.

III   *Oranges*

You broke the blender
With too much spinning:
It sits on the draining-board
With a shred of afterthoughts

About doing dangerous things
With you: I saw the way
You force-fed it with
Oranges from Seville, you

As athletic and young
As any Crawford Art-School girl.
Where oranges sneezed for you
I make a simple, temporary bed,

A ledge where I drink the fresh juice
You made, that gulping treat;
Exhausted lamp in our ceiling,
Scattered rind of bedclothes.

IV   *Your Silence*

When the Italian novelist fell in love with your silence,
With the way you have of keeping things secret:
Well, that was the last straw. Unbearable love, that.
The way you un-gild the lily of yourself, the way
You hide a supreme gift like a child of countryfolk long ago
Running to hide some special gift in a countryside ditch:
That kind of reticence takes seven generations to speak –

So that when you turn to find an escape from praise,
When attention throws you, nearly, into a fit of rage,
I find you can be trapped more deeply in a husband's arms,
Soothed with my well-practised lack of praise, never
Lauded too lavishly. Ah, how you hate the smoothness
Of praise and all of charm's tiresome, inert complexities.

Clothed, unrivalled, secret, how Italian your gifts remain.

V   *Watching the Olympics in a Maternity Hospital*

Exhausted by the effort, you turn your head
To me and I, misinterpreting as usual,
Presume that you are in an ecstasy of motherhood –
A kind of reverse of the mother's grief
In Synge's *Riders to the Sea*,
A female version of those victorious English runners
In *Chariots of Fire* or, indeed, Ronnie Delaney
Falling to his golden knees in Melbourne, 1956.
But as I wipe your marathon runner's brow,
Your maternal face that has trained for this
For years, through coaches and relationships,
Sponsorships, partnerships, pre-nuptial jumps –

You explain in a whisper 'It's oxygen.
It's a lack of oxygen. I need to sleep. Right now.'

A gentleman in a white coat taps my shoulder.
'Here!' says our Lord Killanin. 'Here's her gold.'

VI *Shower*

Beads of water fall from you
When you move between pine doors.

It is the hour after making love
And the house, with its kettle

Singing, its towel crumpled,
Allows in the orange juice of Sunday noon.

I think of the insufficient words
For this. Listen, words are hopeless right now,

Water clings to your beautiful self
The way we clung to our lives

Before we were strong enough to hold together
More than two metres apart. Showered woman,

The day glows like a young cigarette
Before us both. Your coffee is coming.

Our Greek Betrothal

Imagine my great happiness that Thursday
At Mallow Mart, your father telling
John Mannix where he'd missed a bit of concrete
With the hose, hot water getting in

Through the broken soles of my Dunne's shoes;
Imagine how good it was after our chat
About the future of Irish agriculture,
To come to an agreement with your father, Tim,

About the small field I owned near Cappoquin.
If you own a field you can have her, your
Own father said. *Take her away from that fool
Of a lawyer, every lawyer I knew was a Labour pimp*

*Who broke ankles at indoor soccer instead of hurling –
With a good man one field will lead to another.*
So I had no fear taking you away from your patrimony.
It would be three against one, a fair fight.

But the field I owned was far away in Greece.
(See, I fooled even your father!) And so, each year
Since 1982, I send him our first pressing of olive oil
As a son-in-law's tribute, and a kiss from his daughter.

Poetry like Lavender

Your cats make a warm nest, a Persian mother,
Out of lavender. On warmest days of the year
Cats recognize its verticillate heart, its ointment
Of spikenard; of Syria bathing in revenue.

When I smell it I walk on air with 'Our Saviour'.
And you, when you lose your voice, you take two
Spoonfuls of distilled blossom. Your soul should yearn
For this blue scent of the Euphrates: it is paint

Of porcelain, it is a vehicle of colour.
All griefs and pains of the heart and mind,
Each cold cause of suffering, are scented away.
Odiferous, cats recognize its oil of Evangelists:

Lavender like poetry, then, *lavandula spica*,
That is so often applied to the hard world's weather –
Touch its subtle spirit, its essential life,
Such potent and spiky cures. Such mercury!

At the Grave of a Southern Poet

Time dreamed we might be famous together, so it did,

That you would kick the stagnant water-butt, you would tumble
The half-filled salt-cellar and shake all the iodine out of life;
You would be drenched by youth and gulp all the air –

Just new to the city, settled in your river-side apartment,
You dreamed of becoming a cauldron of fame,

Though it was time went up in smoke, poetry that settled
    like embers.
There was *Humboldt's Gift* on your bare stairs.

Now I stand here and look at the dead hand of the dead –

You have returned to earth and its thousand anthologies,
Death has edited you in. You are with *The King of Asine*,
You are adored by all of them, by Seferis

And Pablo Neruda. Those of us who live on, live on fragments.
Dear poet, middle age has made novelists of us all;
We grow old in the city and cannot get settled in –

I am tending still to the slow water-divining of our own
    good ideas;
Faithful to your youth, the shaken salt, the lacking South.

At Fudan University

Three girls who are as mad as hatters about Irish life,
Who studied Oscar Wilde, who sing *The Cranberries*,
Whose eyes are as blue as the sea off the Aran islands:
All approach the podium for a better glimpse of me,
Or not me, but the country that spoke to them
When I spoke. It is strange to come from the distant past;
To be too short-sighted for a full report,
To report upon a kind of music although tone-deaf.
Now, I see all of China dancing, light-footed, expectant,
And clothed in denim. These girls toss the coinage
Of Shanghai at our feet, newly minted,
Twirling across the floor, brilliant; metallic. I think
Of their grandfather, Mao, and their mother, History.

Dave Brubeck at *M on the Bund*, Shanghai

A cloud of sunlit forsythia crashes against glass

This idle and unprepared Palm Sunday:
Quintet brushes of gold, frantic as Dave Brubeck,
Sidle across the window.

The cool cats move closer, waiting for the sun to dance
As it does each Easter. The dust of spring
Makes all of Shanghai sneeze, hurtling mixer and crushed

Ice closer and closer. Give the singer a kiss,
The forsythia says, aggressive with yellow.
Not too far away, but beyond the crowded terrace,

A reception is prepared for the crown of the year.
The sun will be king, messiah and Central Committee,
Ascendant in the sky as each hour goes by;

The hour that expands to hold us, the egg
Of a Chinese Easter beneath our yellowy blossoms.
It is the river Jordan stays far away; it is the song,

Flamingo, and all the other promises
That enter this glamorous bar covered with palm leaves,
Or words carried on a tray of cocktails: *I Never Know*.

Shanghai Days

Another skyscraper: fire-crackers explode across a building-site,
Dispelling all the evil spirits before concrete is poured.
We should have dispelled the spirits before building in Ireland
Or understood the failed *feng shui* from our great Famine height.
We should have seen the startled silverfish, or heard
The dead wailing for caution. Now I see Shanghai at night
With the eyes of an ESB engineer, loving every coloured glass,
    every clean
Steel rampart. Here is the company of humankind,
The harbour where the un-dead congregate. Our of sight
Of troubled Ireland, ferries cross to Pudong's treasure island.

2

Difficult to know how we speak, culture to culture –
It is possible that I connect with China as a Friendship Store,
And that only, or an exhausted stranger in the house of Mao,
Or a youth who loved memories of the Yenan Forum; wanting
    more
Of central planning, wanting more translation, wanting more
Of Arthur Waley. In all honesty, it is difficult now
Not to be an Anglican missionary or an Oblate Father.
Shanghai is so beautiful and complete in spring,
Walking behind a kilted piper, laughing, singing;
All incongruous as St. Patrick's Day in sunny Shanghai.

Our Second Visit to Shanghai

I study the fallen leaf. Not the vivid colour of the young
But time that swirls in its Chinese corner, time
That settles with all the depth of purple. It is death
That teaches her to be sensational, to be a mulberry tree;
To be silk with grief. I have been in love with this widow,
    Mrs. Life,
Since the age of seven. Now her huge retrospective has opened

In the Expressionist Gallery downtown. It is an embarrassment
Of glass and steel, my love that could express itself
Like a studied, elderly poem. What is burnished and of age:
What has the wind and rain made of such an October roof?
A ruined greenhouse creaks in the dark. Tell me again,
Mrs. Life, about wisdom, about grapes with a coating of fur.

Here, it is time that has four hundred and eight names, the
    seasons
With thirty double names of the *Po chia hsing*. I prepare to
    meet life,
Thus attired with my well-earned *kuan ming*. Fully clothed,
I shall trespass like an indifferent, slightly drunk Irishman –
Though it is the fallen leaf that makes a report
To heaven, not any foreign ship at the Pagoda Anchorage.

Study, therefore, October falling in Shanghai and its remnants
    of ink,
Entire inky years unrolled slowly for sheer enjoyment;
The Shanghai highways, the glass and steel of phenomena.
Here, therefore, is *Mrs. Life*, the palm plantations
Of the West River delta, the flow without enjambment –
That one sensational gallery, the poem: the widow's child,
    China.

Del Mar Fairgrounds, 1935

Why you came back to County Waterford
After so much happiness in Del Mar
I shall never understand –

Sitting in Mossy Noonan's Pub,
Listing all the beautiful boiled sweets
Beneath the canvas awnings of

Del Mar Fairgrounds or simply
Cycling to Maddens' in Lismore
In the hope of glimpsing Fred Astaire,

Was how you spent two-thirds of your life.
You saw something in California, Dinny,
That filled your soul. It was sweet enough

To boil the mist off the Blackwater. It was
Even more sublime than a constant blue sky:
It covers you in maple syrup where you lie.

A Commentary on the *Collected Poems* of W. B. Yeats

I was sitting near the Forum of Augustus,
Happy enough in the early winter sunshine
Watching the young and well-dressed of Rome.
A man could be taken aback by the beauty of it –
Such a scene of flowers and heroes.
Here, the young wear youth like a mask,
A perfectly fitting mask, as they enter the room
Of your stare. It is always the Via Botteghe Oscure.
The Princess Caetani is waiting here.
Sit with me awhile, let the words tempt you
For the word has the most perfect breasts
Of men and women; such desires as holiday
Within us when we sit in the long Roman sunlight;
It is such a desire of words that looks to the river:
That forum of flowers and Victor Emmanuel.

Which is why it is now so strange
That as I share this mild coffee with my own poem
An elderly man of silver hair and sallow skin
Lays an ivory-handled walking stick
On the light chintz of the café table,
And follows with the book of my misspent youth,
Jeffares' *Commentary* on the poems of Yeats:
A Stanford edition of 1968,
Green cover, yet low-budget, plain and reticent.

Old Grandpa Yeats, the heroic endurance of all that,
The history of it, the lapis lazuli, his damp Irish rage:
And the page opened upon a note on 'that great Queen,'

As Hesiod told and Jeffares explained, Aphrodite,
Born from the sea, derived from *aphros* or foam –
Aphrodite cast upon the café table, still fatherless.

Poems of the Desert

1 *At the Time of the Balfour Declaration*

Or sometime later, certainly before the Paris Conference,
Because my younger brother had just disappeared
Into the man-eating quicksands of Umm al Samim.
I remember that day in the Rub' al-Khali, that desolate
    emptiness
Where quartz and feldspar converse with the Holy Prophet.
Blessed be the names of *Cornulaca Arabica*, of *Danthonia
    forskallii,*
Of all words that make a flower of the blood-red sands:
That's what the strangers said, Mr. Chang Ch'ieng and Miss
    Freya Stark,
As they gulped from our goatskins, the Imam advising them;
Night-time coming; prayers over: a collision of interests –

Not your war-machines, the Imam said, Miss Stark taking
    notes,
Nothing the West can throw at us, but over-grazing –
The eternal un-sharing of the wilderness, the wickedness of
    man.

2 *Bitter with the loss of two favourite books, Mr. Thesiger*

Stopped on the Heddah–Mecca Road, muttering to our camel
The names of everything that is lost in this brief life –
W. A. Bromfield's *Letters from Egypt and Syria* and J. E. T.
Aitchison's *Botany of the Kuram and Hariab districts* are,
Most certainly, a terrible loss in 103^0 of summer heat,
But even the youngest son among all Bedu camel-herders

Could have warned this crusty foreigner, this dried apricot
Of a European, this thorn on the bark of an acacia tree,
That here we are far from the scarlet-fruited *abal* or the *hadth*
Saltbush. Down on his luck, he asks me yet again
To describe my Arab boyhood, the nocturnal moths
Drinking nectar of Abutilon on a late spring evening;

And in May, *Rosa abyssinica*; the white splash of flowers.

3   *Mr. Wilfrid Scawen Blunt Attacks an Akabah Shark*

It may have been an obsession with the Khedive Ismail's reign,
Or anger at waste in the Viceregal Kiosque of the Pyramids
Or Cavagnari's tragic death in Kabul, Lytton's new war,
Or the ghost of his *Secret History of the English Occupation of
    Egypt*,
But his killing a curious shark from a well-known shoal –

A shark from a shoal as pro-Western as Sherif Huseyn Ibn Aoun;
In these lustrous waters, constantly grazing the boats,
Scattering a sea of vermilion, purple and gold –
His greeting this ten-foot shark with a fatal blast of buckshot
Was unfair to a fish that leaped merely to look closely at the West.

4   *They were friends of Colonel T. E. Lawrence*

Or so they claimed when we met them at the railway junction,
The fuse already lit and dynamite hidden in the sedge,
A troop-train of the Ottoman Empire fast approaching,
Our own Sheikh screaming at me to get down, get down,
You absurd Assyrian shepherd, get down or die like a fool:

But I was distracted by the two strangers on camels,
Two poets of the far Oceans, Irishmen, volunteers from the
    West,
Like the catastrophic Munster Fusiliers of Baghdad –
Captain Desmond O'Grady and Lt. James Clarence Mangan,
Who, dismounting, grumbling like their far-travelled camels –
We want to be sure, they said, sure of the Arabic word for
    'home.'

A Waterford Boyhood, 1963

Between the perfect *blah* you brought home from Barron's shop
And the smell of four large bottles of Smithwicks on your breath

I escape, dear father, with the agility of a startled deer.
It's not that I'm ashamed of anything you represent; it's not

The old NSU bike with the chains loose in their rusted cage,
Or the shoulder of young ash stolen from the Major's field;

For the world of bike and shoulder had taught me long ago
Just how far in the little world of Cappoquin we'd sunk –

No, unhappy sir. But it was something else, call it my poetic hour,
If you like. Now, I'm talking about something before books

And let me be as plain as possible about this, no camouflage,
No myth-making. To put it quite simply, I was a frail boy

Having dreams beyond me on my father's disability book;
The way you had dreams too, but without a borrowed thesaurus:

Why I escaped, while the neighbours were moaning about
        injustice,
Was that I heard Lady Keane calling to me from the orchard gate.

---

blah: a small loaf of bread in Waterford City
shoulder: a length of generally stolen timber

Stoat and Kestrel

I was minding my own business playing with this inky
New fountain-pen, scratching quietly as I'm wont to do
In the spinsterish manner of a European poet;
Scratching leisurely hieroglyphics on my day off.
The evening crawled slothfully towards my window,
A parthenocarpic poem approached its anaerobic hour,
When out of the blue (well, blue dulling to coal dust),
A kestrel tore out of the screeching sky, its aluminium
Hinges lunging to earth. I hadn't noticed a hunter
Abroad, nor its four-legged victim in the hot grass
Now snatched from the undergrowth in a reflex of talons –
Nor had the kestrel, it seems. For what it spied as a rat
Was nothing as fat; rather, a livid hunting stoat
Suspended quickly in an electric sky, a twisting killer
That severed its flying jugular. Their deathly cloudburst
Tumbled to earth. Thump! Both creatures dead of themselves –
Now, I put this pen away. And the evening, so un-Irish,
So ironic and post-modern in its lack of a funeral,
Withdraws from the incident; the fertile hour blue as ink.

A Polish Youth Thinks Only of Home

I mention Milosz and the more mysterious Szymborska
And, not getting any nod of recognition, I try 'Conrad' –
He *must* know him, that migrant with three native tongues –

But there's silence still in the late afternoon café.
Then I tell myself, in that welcoming, reassuring manner
I have, for I've always had a great Irish welcome for myself,

That hard work is a great thing, and, of course, cheap airlines:
And, come to think of it, great famines. Sure, didn't we
Have a Great Famine ourselves in the days before Ryanair?

But there's still no connection. *Celtic Tiger*. Plenitude,
The long journey of my cake-crumbs from table-top to apron:

Eat, he must mean to say, *I'm here to work. Get over it.*

Hiding Joseph in Ireland

It is too complex now to be telling you the full story
And anyway I know you and I know what you'll do:
You'll put Joseph in a poem just as we're trying to
Help everyone to forget Joseph. He never lived here.
We don't know. We don't know. What does it matter
To you whether it was Rwanda or Burundi or Sudan,
Whether it was another small place in a pool of oil,
A place somewhere in Nigeria that caused Joseph
To flee. *Does it really matter to you?* I mean,
God forbid, you seem to understand only politics.
As for Joseph, let me tell you he can rhyme in his third
Language better than you could do in your first.
We loved the lecture you gave us on the Celtic poets,
How they spent seven years in apprenticeship. It
Was the same with Joseph. I don't wish to embarrass
You, but he spent seven years keeping a rhythm of exile,
And when he found his father, and two brothers,
Dismembered, covered in a cloak of crude oil,
He knew the apprenticeship was over. In this way
He learned about poems. He has fled to keep his hands.

September Refugees

The long electric line of refugees at the Western Union counter
Rumbles quietly in a shuffle of feathers

The way song-birds shuffle on a pillow of wires
As they receive the few coins in late September sunlight.

This is the hour of putting away every thought of drowning.

An open boat that carries you through this life;
Impenetrable terror of the North Atlantic,
Misery of head-winds, weakness of the will to live:

Be a survivor, the counter-clerk of the wind says. Be a song-bird.

Because I can't tell you what you feel, in this line of low
        conversations,
I can only see the wound of the world bleeding into me.
The wound is no longer Cuchulain's wound, forget that:
Here, I can place my hand in a wound in Ireland now –

I can only tell you what I feel when I see you assembled
On the high autumnal wire of the Minister's office;

But here is Ray Lema being born on a train in Zaire,
Who came out of the womb singing 'Lusala,' 'Lusala,'
And here, Pierre Akendengué's persistent rain in 'Silence,'
        'Silence.'

Flock and sing. Survive. We met once before, you know,
We made love and good marriages in another South.
But this is not the time to talk, not yet. A time will come

To be together around a family that sings, as music is our best
    word.
This is the first morning of a wind-borne homecoming,
Shuffle of survivors, voyagers, mothers with the strongest will –

As when the Willow Warbler, in late September,
Begins to sing again in a sudden, irrepressible outburst of hope.

Full Moon over the Refugee Centre

This is what it takes to come into your own kingdom,

To stop banging your head against a liberty tree,
To take something strong for your national headache
And find others around you, heads split open:

This pilot's moon that shines on a free Europe
With all the glamour of remembrance,
All the night-drops, wireless signals, replayed *Casablancas*,
Shines also upon the Kinsale Road Refugee Centre;

An inexhaustible moon it is
That scatters across the sky its silver, untranslatable dust.

Brief Encounter with Miss Sochima

Exile has set me to reading like my teachers never could.
There is so much to learn as a refugee; and the
                                        Consequence
Of not knowing fills me with an urgent dread.
                                        Like you said,
I will never get a fair hearing in Ireland
Until I stop expressing pain and make a poem instead –

Last Wednesday, for the fourth hearing of my case,
Our distracted judge mumbled a beautiful poem by Yeats,
                                        keeping his eyes
On the finely printed page, instead of looking at my face.

A Photograph of Paul Engle, 1978

for Hualing Nieh

It's been thirty years since I walked on Dubuque Street
Last time I saw Paul Engle I was twenty four.
Now I pick him from a desk that is scarred with age.
He fell into this, my writing moment, from a page

Of Richard Wilbur's *The Mind-Reader*
That I bought in Prairie Lights one snowy day.
It was the hyphen between Wilbur's *Mind*
And *Reader* that I couldn't leave behind

In that snow-lit bookstore. And Paul fell in with me
As I walked by the Iowa River, defending hyphens
And other tight devices American poets love.
I had come from a place that treasured looseness above

Anything else on earth: looseness of pub life;
Looseness of history and a disjointedness of civil wars.
There was an ocean between me and what I could
Use in poems. Neither of us, reading Wilbur, understood

How a photo and a memory picked off the desk
Could join me to my first days in Iowa, could hyphenate
Us both into a compound afternoon of snow and home –
Or how such hyphens linked unwritten poems to come.

Thames Clipper to Your Wedding

for Peter and Tatiana

This evening all of London is an oriental scarf, flecked
    cochineal.
The water is red also, and the board walk below Greenwich
Becomes alive with light. This is about as peaceful as the earth
    can be
On any Saturday evening. Our hydrofoil skims across Thames
    silk
Like a steam-iron, and the conductor's bourgeois Irish voice,
Soft as a girl's school in Laurel Hill or Rosscarbery, calms
    the crowd –
Who seem unsure whether their stop is Canary Wharf or
    Castletownbere.
The accent is upside down. The tannoy is calm. The water
    is wide.

Dublin

I open our sash window to the inner city sky:
Sunday morning clouds, electronic clang of a great bell
Between the rain-drenched quays and the Gresham Hotel;
Aroma of coffee with water just off the boil

And that distant fluttering, specks of conflict
In the air above us, like Lavery's German bi-planes
In that great painting from the First War, dim frames
Caught in lighted haze, painting their frail aspect

As they bank and turn. And then, that great Dublin call,
Uniquely Dublin, the squeal of Norah MacGuinness sea-
Gulls as they lift off the canvas of her closed gallery:
The sheer beauty of it, this cacophony as her gulls fall.

Dissident Poet

Five times in this life I tried to escape from Fianna Fáil:
The first, while I was still a very green teenager
And seeing a girl from the Lismore Dáil Ceanntar.
Her mother came to fetch us from behind the Eighteenth Dáil –

Next time, I fell head over heels in love
With a young Maoist from Macroom. Black-
Haired and wild, she brought politics and art
To life, but would do only what Chairman Mao approved

In his long speeches at the Yenan Forum.
Next I was swayed by Conor Cruise O'Brien's attacks:
But Jackie Fahey T. D. had been to Katanga and back
Many's the time, he said, and so I came to no harm.

Then it was Faiz Ahmed Faiz when I was twenty four,
The two of us sitting in Iowa, dining on Jameson and oats:
You will never win a Lenin Prize chasing ghost-*cumann* votes:
Think revolution, Faiz advised. And I was nearly won over.

But what did it in the end was a long afternoon
At IMMA, that Labour refuge, an enclave where a soul could
        hide –
There I fell in love with the chthonic strokes of Lucien Freud,
His asylum of paint; his promise that poets could begin again.

A Fianna Fáil Adoption

For years I kept it from my parents that I'd adopted them –
Adults being frightened of the raw truth, as you know.
They were simple people after all, and barely hanging on
To the edge of life. Working class

                    and doubly cursed

With residence in a town of shifting constituency lines,
What did they know of the great national issues at hand?
In my pre-natal career I'd been with Ben Briscoe
And Lemass when they hand-picked

                    the two thousand men,

Yes, men, who would be the backbone of every *cumann*.
I knew at the time they were keeping an eye out for moral girls
Who might become my mother. But they were busy then
And I spent most of my time in Lemass's

                    glove compartment,

Only emerging now and again when I heard a brass band
Or the distinctive flash of a press-photographer's camera.
I grew into life loving election crowds and the smell of burning
    tar.
You must understand, I never had a worry

                    in this pre-natal car.

Only when the Party got a terrible fright after the last war
And the State of Emergency was still maintained, did Lemass
Leave me behind in Cappoquin. It was in Walsh's Hotel
That the Party Chairman picked me off the

                    wide window-sill

That faces Olden's Shop. 'You need to be born at once,' he said,
We need new blood in Fianna Fáil.' It was then he saw
An effervescent girl of the Tobins and a boy home from the war
In Rineanna; and he arranged,
                              with Condolences Dineen,

Then the very proud owner of a Ford saloon, to have me
        delivered
While these two impoverished creatures made love. And so it
        was
Difficult for me, growing up among factory labourers and
Men who thinned sugar-beet, to keep our
                              great nation in mind

Until I was fourteen and found, once more, Condolences
        Dineen –
He knew what to do. 'Learn the bit of Irish,' he said, 'Don't
        forget to join
The GAA.' I kept such connections to myself, growing every
        day, but
What wrecked the magic
                    was my mother's virulent poetic strain.

Ireland, 2007

We've almost come to the end of our poetry of whining.
It is difficult to whine for the disappointed consumer,
Locked-out in the late July rain, whining.
That *Not a Plastic Bag* bag was a limited edition
But it's not exactly like missing the Famine ship, whining
In despair at Fenit pier. And that HD screen you missed
Will come round again. Believe me, it will. The global
Sales-force knows your address, just like the whining
Landlord's sheriff who sent you packing with a Notice to Quit
In 1882. But what has me furious, what has me whining
Still, is the loss of out telephone network to Babcock
And Brown Inc. It is not famine and exile, but this whining
Utility Bill, that makes me want to find the Croppy's Pike
Hidden in the unwired attic. Someone will pay for this price-hike,
This asset-stripping. Guess who'll pay, you ask, whining.

Library Triptych

1 *Her Book of Hebrew Prayers*

Well now, it was a soft rain fell on Israel, that October day
When summer did a somersault away from us and climbed
Aboard the great express of the seasons. Mr. Goldberg
Was well into his happy term as Lord Mayor, and Sheila,

His beloved, was arranging flowers on the new Steinway:
Everybody was so young, though I was older at the time,
But just at a point where I might have begun my life again,
Full of a hope like Mr. Goldberg had. A rash of poems

Had begun to pepper magazines, a girl had come in
For Françoise Gilot's book and took me instead:
Impossible hope among the books farthest from the door;
Endpapers on the bare floor, intermittent smell of dope.

Everything connected, like our earliest notes for a poem.
There was an acidic and sexual rain. Far away in the poor
      suburbs
A struggling pensioner climbed aboard our Mobile Library
And placed a damp prayer-book into my outstretched palm –

A book of Hebrew prayers; a family heirloom
More valued, even, than William Bulfin's *Rambles in Erin*.
It had fallen to the wet street. No matter, Mrs, your mother's
Memento of a lover in New York: it is only soft Irish rain.

But today it's more ER Librarianship; a new borrower
With a black eye falls through the section on poetry,
His teenage sister, with his tickets in shreds, roars
After him that he'd better watch his second eye

If he ever lays another hand on her very best friend.
At the checkout a mother takes aim with her phone
And Nokia submits to a test of broadband,
Flying through Self Help, to hit a book on migraine

And miss the child: now, rushing, breathless, troubled,
Mothers scramble for books in the children's section –
For them parenthood is not a romantic book company:
Rainy afternoons chain them to pillars of children.

It is raining outside, yet again. Uniformed children
Blow manuscripts against the wet window-glass.
Impromptu pictures form of their absent fathers;
A misted loneliness is what their sleeves wipe clean.

I zap the codes, think of the breathless woman who bore me –
My own desolate mother, in a bleak town full of men,
Calling for her family. I understand, now, a mother's
Love, its endurance like the incredible patience of the rain.

Spines of the *Irish Builder* exhale in wax contentment,
Almost sundown and a dulled peroxide of light
Drags a quilted cover across curtained, quarto journals:
As if the early eighteenth-century past that holds

All our bindings would suddenly dissolve and part,
As if books were not important; as if the unseen efforts
Of our best binder and her well-chosen apprentices
Meant nothing in the long and deliberate time taken

To hold and save each book when penetrating rain
Seeps through this wreckage of a 1970s breeze-block
And glass repository: as if design meant nothing:
Time itself places its architect's delicate long fingers

Upon this small matter of decay. A moth disturbed,
Time: paper is stamped with the winter-mark
Of our repository, a bloom peels from the fruit of these
Pages. You wouldn't believe the firmness of time

As it calls a meeting with books and periodicals –
Even as they leave, erratic newspapers applaud
Loudly in their bins, like so many amazed librarians;
And the dead applaud: those Maltons, those Hobans.

Atonement

Blackberries fall like a purple snow as I hack
Away: such layers of neglect coming apart in tears,
Such remnants as hang around endings.
This is not the New Year as we knew it
But these first days of September,
Three of our household outdoors, two on ladders
Hacking away, cutting back the unpicked fruit
Of a long wet summer. The yard echoes
To the crash of a lopped sycamore, a bucket
Is flipped from its moulding perch, our two cats
Erupt in a fury of tufts. This, really, is new –
Not the year, then, but our efforts at atonement
Before the Talmud turns nasty above uncut grass,
Before the year says something about being unloved.
And, so. You bring a green tray of steaming teas
Like the mother in Anjelica Kaufman's high art:
Such boyish effort to begin again, such Yom Kippur.

The Protestant South

*Be thou faithful unto death, and I will give thee
a crown of life.*

— REVELATIONS XI

Because I've no business describing the Protestant
South, I feel like describing it all over again
Having seen the flower arrangements at Carrowdore:
It is a ridiculous hope and no obligation
Of mine to catalogue flowers while the language burns,
But there is something fatally attractive
In a small enclave, of above average height,
That hovers subtly over cut flowers and cut stones.
Here, I peel away the lacquer, fretwork and inlay
Of a not insignificant people, to reveal a fury
Of enterprise, something that has both
A distinctive style and the wherewithal to praise God.
Because of these cut flowers I now lift the lid
On a different assembly, and, arriving in Cork,
See that it is Cork's particular sensibilities I note
In the arrangement of history; in things that set us apart.
As there are Gallweys and Lawtons to trade
So there are others who merely look on and marvel
At the wealth of ladies, the La Touche banknotes,
The very art of Italy that folds into a Penrose.
It is Mr. Burchell lighting the last boiler at Bandon Co-Op
Before setting off to England to fight his war;
It is the Swanton sisters, leaving Douglas Village
On two manly motorbikes, heading for Ballykinlar Camp;
It is a West Cork farmer covering a bridge in Pothus Wood.
It is a ridiculous hope to get inside a frame
That is strong enough to hold only the burden of flowers.
With this hurling-stick of a pen I could break glass
And disturb the settling peace of things. Here, I place

Those elements of Irish life in my green pipette
And shake and shake. Though I hear nothing
Shattering, I can hear the creak of a bamboo chair
As it settles in a book by Elizabeth Bowen,
I can hear the clink of a glass in Molly Keane, the sharp
Edge created by an attractive rival: the sound of horses
Cantering over winter ice. And here, listen, the creak
Of ordinary Protestant life as it angles away
On a bike, a High Nelly that Miss Cliffe used
To spend a summer's morning in Dungarvan,
Miss Cliffe who kept to the edge of William Trevor's
Prose, whose world was old ledgers and glass jars:
Though it is always October, leafy Lismore weather,
That she cycles into, mostly leaf-mould, remembrance –
Carrowdore, then, and the select vestry of poets,
But across the yard, almost overlooked, the work
Of Carrowdore women, the sheer pluck of flower-arrangement
In the face of striking poems; how when we have
No business with techniques of verse, and no license,
We can still make sense with a florist's best stock.
There is not more than trimmed euphorbia between the poem
And the poet: that, dear Bishop MacNeice, was their message
To your bright BBC son. Wild fuschia
May cover his grave, but the world is as the son ordained,
A snowfall of gypsophila florets, carefully framed.

Trains

Manager,
Please put the Snows of Kilimanjaro on
the 4.15 Mallow train.

       — TWENTIETH CENTURY-FOX, DUBLIN

You can hardly imagine the tunnel of growth
In adult life, life so different from the spray of cow-
Parsley on a late summer railway embankment,
A shower of whiteness that asked me to be a pen

To write some childhood's meaning upon it.
You were not there, Miss Coakley; but up the line,
Where all the good news came from, you were
Being born of a graceful mother. No engineer

Called across the line, no linesman smelling of creosote
Tapped at my shoulder, saying 'There is a love for you!'
For there were years to go before you stepped
Down from a carriage on the Mallow line, articulate

With cameras and stones, carrying a dancehall raffle-card
With my name embossed therein. I was not seeing anyone off
But struggling to face the music for such long absence
From home. But the embankment had foreknowledge

Of my life, in a slanted, inarticulate way,
And the sleepers, points and great parasol of wild flowers
Were ready to speak for me. My good name was assured
On this childhood embankment, assured as I raced

With a *Twentieth Century-Fox* aluminium box
Through a thicket of summer growth
To reach the train that I could hear in the distance,
Blowing hard below Glenshelane Wood, too close for my good,

But still the train, the *very* train, that we needed
To carry this valuable box with the week's feature film
All the way to Mallow Junction. Film had a child's
Meaning upon it, but this child's meaning only –

Rolling-stock coming to its grinding hour, doors
Sliding to receive my treble-docketed aluminium and strap.
'Well done, lad.' A deep baritone, a guard
So full of strength and so unlike my father

That I was sorely tempted to climb aboard.
No, not yet. I needed to climb more slowly through
Loneliness, get to know it without its burdens,
Its embankment of cow-parsley and railway-dockets,

Without meaning, yet. But you can still see,
If you look closely for traces of a provincial train,
Those patterns of replenishment and retreat;
Railway movies carried by a child, no other reserved seats.

Athens, 2005

for Joe Gavin

Emblems of the Hellenic world of trade, *Ionian*, *Olympic*,
    a Byronic *BA*,
Cruise past the waiting windows, touch down, gate or
    disengage:

Each European driven to Ithaca, each creaking console
    turning to complain
Of its burden of suitcases, each with a Mediterranean
    assignment.

My suitcase falls like an exhausted marathon runner at the
    gate of Athens:
The flight attendants in smart uniforms tell us to be alert
    and wait.

This is the Europe our fathers could never have imagined as
    they fled
Westward, across the ocean, leaving Queenstown and Genova
    tear-stained.

Behind them, as they fled, entire civilizations were waking
    from a sleep,
An exhausted sleep of wars; a long nightmare of occupations.
    Europe was

Never as alert as this, not in our lifetimes nor in the lives of
    our fathers,
Alert with untaken journeys of pleasure, as full of its own
    trade

As the quaysides of Boston or the blue furnaces of Philadephia.
I think of those journeys out of something. A flight out of
    Europe:

The spars creak and the sea folds and unfolds to remonstrate
    with time,
To show its wrists to the wind; to show its broken chains to
    the sky

As now the young Europeans show their passports and IDs with
    such
Nonchalance, and lack of interest. The whole of Europe's on
    the move

Again, but this time into itself: the idle moves to the working
    part,
The cold North seeks the hot islands as if Greece could hold
    enough light

To satisfy our darkness. I've just said farewell to the
    companionship
Of the great, to Dora Bakoyannis in Athens Town Hall,

To a beloved Spyros Mercouris speaking at the Pnyx, making
    a promise
To support the work of poets, Spyros who brought Greek
    sunlight

To the Big Screen, who watched Melina become a singer of
    genius,
A genius of phrases, beautiful and nonchalant as a Greek
    cigarette –

So that we wonder what it is we are looking for
And we wonder what the fuss was about, budgets that
    wounded committees,

And wonder too as we sink into the grace and ease of an
    Hellenic life
Where it was our plane journeys began, what politics and foul
    weather

Made us board our plane of exile, this sun charter called
    Capital of Culture,
And I think of the Hellenic canvas of James Barry, and how
    it all began;

Not to mention, in passing, the Hellenic ideal of Europe in
    our scholars,
W. B. Stanford's book, the songs of Father Prout, etc., etc.,

Or whether our plane took flight much later than that; in
    our father's time,
The Berlin Airlift, the harrowing films of the Holocaust and
    the vileness

Europe is capable of; or Melina Mercouri's dream, her
    idealized place
Where a child might grow tall with European-ness, at home
    and in love

From the Shannon river to the Danube Volga, or Vistula;
    consoled
By culture for all the horrors of war and exile . . . Until quite
    suddenly

I see, clear as a glass of water from the Nagle Mountains, a ragged
Child, a little gypsy boy or a child coming home from a Talmudic
    lesson,

I see that child grab his one precious suitcase, a cardboard case
    marked 'Europe',
And all my hopes go with him, all the cut-stone, the undiscovered
    treasure.

Molly Keane Considers Brigadier FitzGerald

I am sitting here by the sea with a bunch of thyme,
Quiet as the stranger who held a wreath for Harry Lime.

It is as cold as Vienna in October Ardmore,
Rosemary in my hand wonders what I'm remembering for.

Let's not remember too much of the last war, or the war
Before, that took so many of the promising and fair.

He picked these herbs in the black market of the first
Frost, rushing about as October did its worst

In the hilly gardens at Glenshelane. The last chives,
Clipped back from bolting, are so like the half lives

Of boys who came home in mufti. The astrakhan
Of his collar was neatly re-attached by Ann

But is peppered, still, with an embedded thistledown.
Time comforts us both with its godly motion,

Time stains champagne with its peach liqueur;
This bouquet is a Bellini of sorts. Only the war,

And the wars and the wars men must want to fight
Come between the Vienna of day, Ardmore of night.

An Anglo-Irish Luncheon Party

I was with my father chasing the last seven votes,
Like a young curate of the old school delivering Repeal cards,
When this party of the *Belle Assemblée*
Passed us by near Lismore Bridge. It was
A procession like no other; it was

Fine women carrying the torch of life –
Look at 'em, said my father, a luncheon meeting
Of the one and only Distressed Women's Relief Fund.
History is silk, grief is a watercolour;
Death in such company is a black bead from Vesuvius.

My father and I let them pass by: Lady Keane, a Miss Musgrave,
The late Mrs. Wyse, Miss Healy and others. It was all
Egyptian red cloth, pomegranate blossom, barbel-blue,
Turquoise-stones, a Glauvina pin, a velvet Bolivar hat.
I thought upon our own ornaments that we carried –

Two Party cards, two ash hurling-sticks, two copies of *The Nation*:
How such ornaments glittered for us in a different light!
An ornate bridge was trimmed with olive-green trefoils of satin,
The Cappoquin road wore a strict Court mourning. Each to
     her black
Scarf of barège silk, my father said: each to her fallen.

Part Two

The Last Geraldine Officer

At Templemaurice House

In the beginning, light. At Templemaurice House,
Light in the cool dust of Nineteen Nineteen –
A grid of morning on the bare floorboards,
Oak light and ivy light, and the lead-crystal green

Of a Waterford demesne. Immense dreams
Coagulate around my fretting childhood heart:
My father dead in the Great War, a lost Geraldine.
His books and manuscripts practise their art

Upon me and upon his loyal servant on earth,
My Uncle Walter. Dear bothered Captain FitzGerald
Paces the attic floor above me, learning poems
At dawn as he has always done; wizard Earl

Of the Irish language, eccentric patron of the House.
A language. A poem. A Captain's drum-beat stirs,
Disturbs the dust. The grandeur of the world
Enfolds me still. Immensities. Cries. Open doors

And doors closing in the long corridor, the sound
Of water tanks replenished, the rasp of fire grates,
Mrs. Norah Foley's bicycle in the cobbled yard.
Urgency. Maura's frightened laying of plates –

Ah! I turn in my bed against the full light of day
Like any Irish child spoilt in the motherhood of war.
The U-boat of the hour has passed taking my father,
But I have begun again as the child of Uncle Walter,

Learning Irish faster than he ever could, the *modh*
And *tuisil* call me to themselves, but vex him still.
In the beginning, the immense light of poetry,
The long immortal grid of light from Dromana Hill

That emblazoned the first hour of each private day.
Not simple. Not that. The light shone down upon us
Peculiarly even then; Anglo-Irish light
That shone on Usshers, FitzGeralds, Chearnleys, River Finnisk,

Blackwater and Bride, Dromana and Templemaurice.
In childhood's bedroom, a kind of waiting place:
All the material of what might ever be rushes in;
Poems, fathers, history and breakfast, all find space

And I sing beside them; hum and sing again
My uncle's macaronic anthem, *Na Connerys* –
Too young to know the troubles, Fenian or raparee,
Yet I've gauged the ambient temperature, find ease

In song as if my Geraldine soul was born again
And hidden now in the culvert of a bedroom.
Under bedclothes the diffused light, and all
Bearable things; mother of the house, the womb.

Strange how a boy of nine, hiding naked in dawn
Happiness of himself, how such a lizard creature
Can see the whole of history. Clairvoyant is
Childhood, and complete is the soul's future

In a boy who has buried the father of himself.
The long day goes singing away from me, *tabhair*
Fuascailt orainn araon, like a convict in a convict-ship:
It is the future I must wake to see, to see its power

Racing across the twenty-acre field beneath my room,
Down to the wide Blackwater, the liberating sea.
I part the bedclothes as I parted cold watercress
To slake my thirst. Surface. Norah Foley calling me,

Calling the entire household, but by proxy, with Maura's
Nervous tinkling, an Alpine cow-bell in the wide hall.
In ten minutes we will have assembled by the long table,
Uncle Walter and I, my mother, my sister Nesta, full

Of youthful gossip from her picnic at Glenshelane,
Her dream Lieutenants, her art class at the Misses Keane.
For half an hour Mrs. Norah Foley will cede her warm kingdom
With a pretence of work outdoors: she succumbed to a whim

Of my war-wounded Uncle, allowing the 'quality' to dine
In her kitchen; a kindness that is hidden from each
Big House that corresponds with us from far and near.
Maura serves in silence, with Mrs. Foley out of reach

And out of ear-shot. Only when Uncle Walter primes
With his sword-stick the cobble of the yard does she
Appear once more, armed with a trug of potatoes,
With prodigious leeks, dark chives and fresh-cut parsley.

Deep childhood. Dreams. An older sister to take all the blame:
I was as spoilt a boy as was ever born near Cappoquin,
Retained at the farm, tutored by devoted women, enthralled
By a Captain parcelled home from war, never to leave again.

Templemaurice seemed to dream through me, as Uncle Walter
Did, thrilled by my love of words, of verbs and conjugations:
As months passed in slow time, pictures from *Illustrated War
News* torn down to make way for old poems of *The Nation*

And inexorably a kind of nation was given birth each time
My Uncle, after breakfast, recited a mysterious *Eriu* poem.
Here in the house I made a kingdom of Cuchulainn and
My kinsman, the Wizard Earl. Kuno Meyer and I shared a throne,

With my Uncle as faithful Chancellor. I could hear a deer's cry
And the blackbird in the wood, the monk snoring loudly
And the cock's persistent crow. Each translated image was
A subject that I could see, a deer or a blackbird breaking free.

Add salt to our history, pepper the memoirs of the well-fed,
History is no vichyssoise, so be sparing with the cream;
Heat the butter until it foams, Mrs. Norah Foley said.
Add the chopped nettles in memory of our millions dead.

It is late springtime in the Templemaurice household,
Yellow house in a flood plain by a tidal river at Old Affane.
My Uncle Walter has caught the first trout of the season,
Fish speckled and delicate in his outstretched adult palm.

Mrs. Norah Foley and my mother pace a floor that's cold as slate,
Happy with the glossy greens, adding freckled, first potatoes,
Covering the morning talk of Cappoquin with chicken stock,
Settling the story of each family, stacking them in neat rows

Like my uncle's fresh-caught rainbow trout on the grill.
It is the before-summer of prodigious, elemental growth –
Even my uncle's words flick with a last gasp in the summerhouse;
Salt and words, pepper and poems complete our May-time meal.

Far away in the mist are the chopped scallions of roof-tops,
Farther in their ordinariness from what is happening at home:
Salt and pepper of the Irish language, exceptional love-poems,
'bush-citadels in grey hood', Uncle reads James Kearney's poem;

For he and Mr. Percy Ussher are trawling in the tide of Irish,
Swopping Kearney and Kuno Meyer in the snug at Russell's
    shop.
Along the narrow corridor, between kitchen proper and cobble
    yard
I retrace the footsteps of the family with a child's reversed walk.

That Day of Bereavement

A thunder-clap, waking me at the ungodliest hour,
Has brought me to the window to look the long meadow
In its unmade-up face. Cattle lying in a bovine haze,
The morning haze sheltering like a deer in the willow

And salley ditches, the morning lies beneath me
Like a watermark on dampened paper, a counterfeit
And a light impression. I am too asleep
For the whole of myself to form; mind's counterweight

Has not yet developed. A poet is not born
As easy as that, nor day by day by day can the soul
Be up-ended suddenly by a roll of thunder
To stand at a Templemaurice window, made whole

By the intuition of a war that happened, a father
Somewhere in Europe on a wet October day
Reaching for the sweet deep purple wound of blackberry,
Anxious, as always, to please; to make of war a holiday.

Something else has roused me from the unmapped sleep
Of my childhood, thunder that rattled the old house
And set a grid upon the deep. A bolt of lightning, a Verey light,
Illuminates the farthest tree, unsettles the sleeping cows

And I settle the white shutters into their frail white cases,
Settle myself into some new, more terrible place
As if by some magical paternal telephony my father
Spoke to me. Out of battle he speaks the Irish phrases

And all the grammar and grid and burdened willow
Baskets of his language flow into my childhood room:
Out of the ether he speaks to me, and I know
Of his death long before the small-town telegram comes,

Or before my mother enters, dark-eyed with distress,
To name the unspeakable loss of my own dear father.
Behind her my Uncle entered, shell-shocked with poems,
And Mrs. Norah Foley with a glass of warm barley-water:

My grief granted them the audience our loss required.
But then I turned away, stiff as a frost on linen sheets,
And made to compose my soul. Only Uncle Walter
Waited still, utterly alone, grammatical with grief,

And singing like an old fisherman of the Foleys
At Killahala Pier, tears streaming down his poor face,
He sings the great song of the black Famine in Dungarvan.
Grief makes him a pure lyrical citizen of the Irish race

And I love him dearly from that moment on, a companion
And a fellow poet, sharing grief only with the printed page.
What a fellowship of two we will make, excluding everyone
With a wickedness of poems. Words become the stage,

As real as the farm that surrounds our house, as real
And sheltered and permanent as Whitechurch limestone;
As firm to dance upon. Out of our grief life goes helter-skelter;
Only poems and grammars can call me back towards home.

And so to wander, to dream and wander through post-war years
As if a kind of wicket-gate had opened behind the laurels,
Or the great walls of whitethorn and bamboo had parted
To reveal a secret patch, devoid of the 1920s, uncontroversial.

Grief and barley-water, the taste is with me still,
Moistens my mouth with memory, makes me thirst;
For my poor father held us back until his death: now Walter
And I plant astringent grass where history did its worst,

And history with its herb of language, its hostage cook,
Recycles all the childhoods ever broken by the Great War
And makes another one to collect childhoods yet to come:
Bereavement is what every childhood is waiting for

In days of total war. A cloud-burst, a Blackwater
Downpour sieves the morning against window-glass
And peppers my Uncle's keening hum with something
Bearable. The sound of rain lets our sorrows pass

As sorrow passes over the language and its landscapes;
A chill, a wind, a cloud-burst. And, after rain, to shake
The soul dry, to leave the shelter of a childhood nest –
The moist cloud empties for its own passion's sake

And leaves me with a delirium of grief. Nothing of words
Could restore me ever to a living father, nor sickly
Barley-water, nor the ministrations of my poor sister.
Nothing could hold me but the salt and lime of poetry,

The untranslated grief of the Blessed Virgin
That came through Uncle Walter's lips from distant
Baile an Chuirrínigh. The words *trí leaca Ví Rósa*
Fall upon our valley of blood, fall like incense

On my barley-water and bed. The High King of Heaven
Will receive him, Saint Declan and the Wizard Earl
Will talk to him, soothe him with kisses of Dromana
Templars. In my uncle's recitations death becomes real.

From now on I shall leap from my bed to watch the river;
Its thousands of fish, its noisy colloquy between grief
And poetry. A lonely place reveals itself all at once
And I go to it, fatherless but buoyed up by that brief

Delirium of a thousand poems. In the years that follow
I would watch the *Dartmouth Castle* making her way
Through Campfire sandbanks: fumes and noise on the high
        tide,
A mysterious craft from Youghal, boxes and hay

On the narrow deck, and the tide taking them back again
Through shallows and salley banks; that was a tide
That ebbed and flowed below my childhood. Elsewhere
There was a grotesque war and there my own father died

As he picked early blackberries for his men; always
A Templemaurice thing, an heroic Geraldine sweetness:
His death connected somehow with Mrs. Foley's baking,
With cinnamon and apple, with shallot and watercress,

With every trained and deliberate gesture of life,
So that I could never tell whether grief was a food
Best covered over, layered, re-heated, or consumed
Whole only by those bereaved who understood.

Through childhood I became the great hunter-gatherer
Of the house, saving everything, cooking all,
Accumulating, dressing, portioning and parsing
Everything into small jars. Even the late October wind-fall

Did not escape me. With cold and wet hands, a pannier
Carried briskly in the rain, I hunted for the very last
Globe of sweetness. My father who would never return
Satisfied everything in memory, all hunger and thirst,

All grammar and poems. The great tide below our house,
The river that would never go away, but flooded still
Each winter meadow, seemed an instrument of poems;
Relentless, teeming, between Kilbree and Dromana Hill.

Apricots in Brandy

Home in the long, last summer from jazz-crazed Eton,
I patrolled the long meadow of new Irish books;
Uncle Walter's great harvest from Cork city and Dublin.
It was Ó Rathaille's *Measgra Dánta* and the prose of Yeats

More than anything in farming or Waterford politics
That filled each conversation at dinner or alfresco lunch.
By now the incredible deafness of the War-dead
No longer paralysed the house. Grief hardly touched

The keys of the piano my mother began to play again,
London drawing-room and Gershwin that filled
With early morning mirth a Déise scholar's house.
Her modern music was a glimpse of hope, a kind of child

Through which my mother might continue to endure.
More a scholar's child was I, carrying a leather satchel
To the boathouse sinking under the strain of laurel –
And held together by force of a consciousness so real

That Templemaurice and I were compelled to pay
Attention. A young man could skate upon the atmosphere
Of our Free State forming a bibliography of its own.
Memories and poems came tumbling from each author,

A rooted and Fenian memory, a rival to the Great War.
Leading to the battlefield year of the Eucharistic Congress
Was a force of something gathering: there were yellow buntings
In each churchyard, a distinct atmosphere after Mass,

That seemed to link the Protestant scholarship of
Uncle Walter, Mr. Ussher, Dr. Hyde, to a warmer
Climate and readership: more of Lazio than Ireland.
Into this climate I fell after Eton, though a lost father

And his Great War memorabilia filled my soul:
It was the incense of the war dead that captured me,
Graves and Sassoon and silent Waterford Redmondites
Who filtered home. Intoxicated by such war poetry,

Drowsy with the narcotic of August near Cappoquin,
In love with my father's wardrobe, I chose a uniform.
Nobody pushed me, nor did Uncle Walter say a word except
That it was good to travel before settling down to farm.

That summer was the summer of a wedding in Mrs. Foley's
House, three days of music and song, coming and going,
Gifts from the Templemaurice townland, a weekend
At a warmed-up glebe house near Tramore, and wedding

Cake that Mrs. Foley baked, ice luminous as acetylene.
A hand-picked girl, chosen for young Paax, home at last
After seven years in the Irish Guards. Joy in the house,
A love intrigue. Just how much love I could gauge

One morning before breakfast: sent to the milking shed
To hurry Paax and his young wife, I came upon
A love scene as perfect as the most perfect lyric poem –
Screams of laughter greeted me as I looked on:

There Paax and his beloved Siobhan were half naked
As husband poured a full bucket of breakfast milk
Over his beloved's glistening breasts, Siobhan's head
Thrown back in joy, such intimacy beyond talk

Or recitations; or any kind of love-song. Naked joy.
Earth seemed to enfold them with the warmth of cows.
I kicked the bucket against the door, heard a wet scrambling,
Laughter and swears. We had to milk again, of course,

To save half a bucketful for the waiting house. 'Your
Mother sent me, I didn't mean to interfere'
And the lovers laughed, telling me that I was true,
A true gentleman. But their image haunted me for hours

That day, and for days after I supped with my own desires
Until they were grounded one night in Arland Ussher's
House. There, I supped with Ussher's complex phrases
And his ploughman's dark grammar. But when apricots

Were served in brandy – only then – did I notice
A woman's eyes fixed steadily upon me; hanging on
My every word as if I was the scholar of that night.
I watched her playing with apricots, accepting strong

Brandies, saying nothing, but more interesting,
Suddenly, than all the Irish language of the very old.
When we kissed after dinner our moist calling-card
Was pressed upon each other's mouth. My heart soared.

It was Lady Enid ffrench-McGrath, who'd arrived
At seven in cobalt satin, osprey and abundant furs;
At twenty one, left weeping and companionless in 1917:
Who now crept gently, carrying her candle between doors,

And wished to speak of the matter of Mr. Yeats' poems;
Of the companionship of ghosts, of séances in Maynooth,
And her husband's table-tapping words. She spoke of
Poetry and adolescence, of Alec Waugh's *Loom of Youth*

And the entire lost, whiskey-soaked nature of grief –
All of this declaimed in a too familiar posture,
A candle melting to a brass lip, a bowl of sodden apricot;
Her body illuminated, welcoming, impure and clear.

As water seeks earth, as electricity seeks its conductor,
She fell to my warmed-up naked body, but not before
Placing the last of Arland Ussher's apricots in brandy
On my bedside table. 'A boy must eat,' she whispers,

'A boy from Eton has much eating still to do.'
In double candle-light we make love, and all the while
I listen to ferocious wind, torrential rain,
That detained us at Cappagh House. The wind howls

But Lady ffrench-McGrath makes a greater noise.
Uncle Walter taps upon the door, 'Are you not sleeping?'
'Yes, Uncle, perfectly at rest. Goodnight.'
The Lady trembles, whether from orgasm or weeping

I can't tell, but learn in days and nights that follow
Every subtle message that one woman's body communicates.
We make love in days that follow in kitchens and stables;
Twice by Killehala Pier, once behind Ballysaggart gates.

We make a feast of each other, of natural hairy food,
As voracious as pigs let loose in a yard, as wayward
And wide-eyed. We talk neither of grief or grammar
But of Mrs. Foley's cooking, of scented custard

And preserved fruit, of Dungarvan crab preserved
And late winter rowan jelly. We feast on food talk
And spoon each other through her silk clothes,
So that by the time I reach the Regimental Barracks

To offer my signature I have a kingdom of love
To draw upon, and dreams beyond a boy's imagination.
She followed me to London in those first months,
But I let go, wanting to break with both flesh and nation.

Ulster Tea and Peach Champagne

Dinner at the Midland, a Yacht Club dance at Helen's Bay,
Motoring to Derry to inspect the forts at Lenane and Dunree:
The General says they'll be soon handed to the South.
It was back to Stormont, then, that autumn weekend in '38.

'Bring your uniform,' the ADC spoke, 'prepare your clothes
For a long over-night. Three of Staff already recalled,
It doesn't look good.' At Stormont we listened to Hitler's speech,
Grown quiet with crisis in this hermetic Unionist world:

Can Belfast be protected with Territorials, bricks and cellophane?
Bizarre weeks of crisis, bizarre travelling Chamberlain.
I rush to the Shorts factory, meet a bevy of Harland engineers,
Meetings round the clock for days, all asked to take the strain

Of imminent mobilization. Then Thursday, 29th, stupendous
Relief, a meeting with Hitler, Mussolini coming to tea.
I dine with a uniformed Frances Cole at the Grand Central;
End at the Opera House with a laughing Jimmy O'Dea;

O'Dea who reminds us all of our neutrality in the South,
That Celtic thing, that fringe, that ability to stand apart –
Like my mother and Uncle Walter who have endured
Three wars, who have lost enough. O'Dea's laughing heart

Was still in my head as we meet again on Army stuff
With Henderson and the Governor General, all hearts
Coming down from heights of fear. Meet with friends
Like Patsy Mulholland, Biddy Herman and Rory Chance;

All head for the Lifeboat Ball in a howling October gale.
Ah, Ulster. We inspect the Northants at Ballykinlar,
Then on to lunch at Clandeboye, playing bridge and
Drinking tea and pink champagne. Once again, I motor

To the East Lancs at Holywood, sherry at the Pollocks',
A military affair, except for Frances with whom
I am a little in love. I dream of her through Limavady
And Drenagh, through a driving, torrential gloom.

Nothing doing. Nothing but dream, for her heart is well
And truly spoken for. But my mind inserts Frances Cole
As a poet's love, inserts her between a lost marriage
In London and a desperate human need to be held

In a lover's arms in a time of fear. I take my Uncle's
Irish poems on our Army reconnaissance at Pointz Pass,
Bring early copies of *Gadelica* with Cinn-lae Amhlaoibh's
Excerpts, inspect the South Wales Borderers with Ó Cas-

aide's deadpan translations on the clipboard at Derry.
I remember Callan at the end of May, Father Mac Craith's
Great day of celebration, texts of the Academy and Maynooth,
And my Uncle among scholar friends. The pure grace

Of Irish scholars assembled there, grammar's dignity
Ever as perfect as the discipline of a well run Corps:
And such work of restoration, such salvage of a nation;
Eugene O'Curry, manuscript hunter, at work before

The rest of Europe had woken to the soul of the Gael.
For who should love us if we cannot love ourselves
In the purest forms: memory, manuscript, poem –
A patrimony preserved for a mere 1,250 guineas

Reminds us all, my Uncle said, of the differing values
Of literature and war, RIA and Hodges and Smith,
Those Southern agitators, how a sense of nation deepens
Life, as deep as our Kilkenny ash tree growing in a ditch.

Manuscript discussions, scholarship and summer classes
At Ardmore and Ring, the Irish conversation of grumbling
And growling old Waterford men; mischievous Arland Ussher
At his falling-down house: my own self unable to bring

Full attention to the work of language, feeling as I did,
The grip of a uniform and an Ulster resident's sense of war:
I kept meeting men who were more angry with Yeats than Hitler.
Returning to Belfast I wondered what such anger could be for

And what did it mean? I mean to be his kind of Irish poet;
This great as Yeats must be great, dying quickly to get away
From our machinery of war: poet who drowned in a sea
Of rumours, who saw war coming, who turned his gaze

From ours and struggled down the winding stair. I walk
Away from the Opening of Stormont, Ulster's Parliament,
Only months after he died. Men of his blood everywhere
And yet not of his kind of Ireland. Here I felt honest dissent;

And another attempt at one version of a dissenting country,
A Protestant Monaco of golf and roses and efficient trains.
Can it be possible that our small history has two parts?
Growing in confidence, building a higher, deadlier fence

Against the Celts and Yeatsians, and the assertive Gael.
I meet Ulster's middle-class on rugby fields, at Balmoral
Show, Portora Royal and Royal Ulster Yacht Club
And sympathize with their attempt to build something small

Out of the remnant of a receding Empire. But is it whole
Or merely protest? I ask myself over and over –
Full of admiration for every Quaker school and Linen Hall.
I read Louis MacNeice's *Autumn Journal* from cover

To cover and think of the loose, sentimental hold
Ireland still has on life, as if the business of the world
Was something more difficult entirely. Hard as Ulster,
Maybe, but honourable like Ulster, if the truth be told.

Motoring through the South in the summer of 1939,
I see how the Gael might be disconnected. The Celtic
Realm was ever peripheral, and this year no different
In its headstrong interior. Compared to Belfast's frantic

Will to grow, Imperial province of linen and steel,
The South seemed an idle place. Idyllic, yes,
But idle as the men who sat and chatted in Lonergan's
Tailor Shop. An industrious garden at Templemaurice

Seemed like a little Ulster in the far South. My Uncle
Walter visits Percy Ussher in his pony and trap
And I go with him, chatting *as Gaeilge* for the whole day,
Overwhelmed by their depth of tradition and trapped

Into a fatalistic sense that everything the Irish language
Had to say was already said. I sense them insert
A tradition as something complete and whole, as sure
Of this as an Ulster Protestant's solemn Covenant.

I sit and listen, attend to something out of time
That seventeen years of Independence has already made:
A sense of nation and that nation's little State.
It was then I felt least at home. Going North, I was afraid

That something had parted, some comforting hum
Of Templemaurice and home. A greater task had appeared
In Ulster: a truly honourable war. Within days, at Florence Court
I meet again that mix of military and Harland engineer.

A Warning Order. Army Form G1098 / At last, the day comes. Our phoney war is over. / Battle-dress, Bren guns, an anti-tank rifle for each platoon, two three-inch mortars, ground sheet, mess-tin, clasp knife and lanyard, field dressing, two towels, A.B. 64 and I.D. discs, anti gas shield and ointment, two pairs of laces, one shirt, one vest, one canvas jacket. / Along Birdcage Walk a row of Green Line buses, waiting. Families begin to gather, nervous girlfriends, anxious sons, proud and shouting Irish daughters: *We'll be with ye, Mick fathers! See ye in Liverpool! In Killarney too with Mrs. Herbert and Lord de Vesey. Watch ye're backs for RSM Stack!* / The Pioneer Sergeant's men go stencilling number 2595 on box and baggage and bicycle. / Carriers to be loaded onto 'flats' at King's Cross / Captain Whitefoord still in shock. Lt. Kennedy and Hackett searching for a personal Remington with telescopic sights. No time to fit new tracks or overhaul the engines. / And the ominous warning about man-size packaging, a breaking down of heavy equipment and portioning of stores, harbinger of a fiery porterage, of a watery disembarkation. / Colonel T. E. Vesey at Euston to say goodbye, a Household Regiment goodbye, shoving a case of champagne into the C.O.'s railway carriage. / Now, the night-journey through wartime England / dry biscuit, tea, a squall of Woodbine smoke. Five books only I bring with me, Ó Duinnín's *Foclóir*, Joseph Hansard's *Illustrated Almanack*, Dungarvan, 1873, Father Sheehan's old Waterford sayings, *Aighneas An Pheacaig Leis an mBás*, Harveys' printing of Coolroe, Mountain Castle's Patrick Denn, my Uncle's copy of MacCraith's *Cinnlae Amhlaoibh Uí Shúileabháin*, a gift from Percy Ussher at Christmas, '37. / They speed through a blacked-out England with me. A blacked-out train. / Crush in the corridors. Steam. / Signalling. / Changing tracks somewhere near Carlisle. / Until, half-asleep, we are steaming slowly into Glasgow at dawn, straight down to the King George V Dock. / The *Monarch of Bermuda:* our first war journey.

Captain FitzGerald's Irish Guards Cake
(war-ration recipe)

> 1 lb flour
> ½ lb moist sugar
> ½ lb butter
> 4 eggs
> ½ lb raisins
> Peel
> 1 tsp mixed spice
> 1 tsp bicarbonate of soda

Rub butter into flour, add spice, sugar, fruit etc. Then add the eggs one by one. Beat all together very well and bake about 2½ or 3 hours in moderate oven.

April 15th 1940

Woken abruptly a few days earlier, taken to the War Office without full dress. Someone thought I spoke Norwegian, but great mirth all round when I explained that I spoke only the Gaelic of Irish poems. Then two books were returned that I'd noticed missing, O'Rahilly's *Measgra Dánta* and Father Sheehan's *Sean-Chaint na nDéise*. As I waited in an ante-room for further instructions or permission to leave I came upon that Waterford phrase 'siubhlaig ar a gcoinnleach' or 'walk on the stubble' and I felt again, acutely, the pain of scratched and cut ankles when I walked as a child through the stubble-fields of Templemaurice. Walking the stubble is very like doing duty to a second country. Painful, silent, bloody. / But I was dismissed at 6 am and returned to Second Company, First Battalion, as the Micks prepared for a long journey. What followed was four frantic days. / A blaze of uniforms and hurried meetings / I became a Colonel's favoured messenger between regiment, London District and War Office. Waiting on hard benches, commanded to wait; waiting to command. / How dreamlike it seems. No, not that, not dreams, but nerves, routine, automatic response. / After the purple-dark journeys by train, the four day crossing, our calm climb into the shoulder of Europe, we have arrived at an eerie, gathering light. / Into the far North we have now steamed, two hundred miles beyond the Arctic Circle, the *Cairo*, the *Valiant*, the *Empress of Australia*, twelve destroyers for discreet company, and two Polish friends, *Batory* and *Chobry*, fateful *Chobry*. / Round the Lofotens we go, now steaming southward down the Vaags Fjord, snow like a linen-field, cirrus clouds of eider-duck rising / Now we have entered the long day of the Ragnarokk, war-time of the *Edda*, wolf-time and sword-time.

April 20th 1940

In Pothus Wood / A Guardsman dies beneath a stony outcrop. And I pray into his ear the prayer my Uncle taught me. / *O Christ! You have suffered every agony of the Passion. Firstly was the suffering of Your own fear, the sweating of Your own blood, on Maundy Thursday. Secondly, I pray for You abandoned by the Apostles and Thirdly I pray for Your wounds as the nails pierced Your hands and feet. My Fourth prayer is for the dragging apart of Your limbs. Fifthly, I pray for You left alone on the Cross as a lamb is left to face a pack of wolves and, Sixth, I pray in commemoration of Your dreadful thirst. My Seventh prayer is for the multitude of souls You saw in the mirror of Your suffering; and Eighthly I pray to Your words* Consummatum est *as the strangers gave You but vinegar. My Ninth prayer is for Your own forsaken words 'Father, have You deserted Me?' and my Tenth prayer is for Your own dear cry as the Spirit departed,* In manus tuas domine commendo spiritum meum. *An Eleventh prayer I say in memory of how You spent all Your strength in the service of our Heavenly Father. My Twelfth prayer I remember in honour of Your Body spent of all blood, upon the Cross. A Thirteenth prayer I cry to Heaven for the great wounds placed upon You; wounds so High they reach to Heaven, so Broad they cover the redeemed Earth. A Fourteenth prayer I say for the rending of sinews and flesh, for such wounds reached the height of Your heart and Your soul, and Your soul did call all the Holy Souls from out of Hell itself. My Fifteenth prayer I say in commemoration of the six thousand six hundred and sixty-six wounds You suffered for the common soldier of a King's Household. Christ the King, deliver us. Amen.* / Hold this ground around a dying Guardsman! Hold this ground!

Mr. Brunnock, the butcher from Cappoquin, gave Mrs. Norah Foley this recipe.

> 3 lbs (more or less) of beef for stewing, cut into chunks
> 2 bay leaves
> 1 large or 2 small onions
> 2 tbsps of flour
> Quarter pint of Guinness from any Dungarvan 'large bottle'
> Salt, and a little pepper
> 8 ounces carrots
> 2 tbsps chopped parsley

Heat oil and put in bay leaves. Add beef and brown rapidly. Push the beef to one side and add onions, just soften. Sprinkle with the flour and brown, then add the Guinness. Top up with water to cover, at least the same quantity as the Guinness. Add the carrots and season very well. Bring to boil and cook (braising) in a slow oven (160° C) for about 1½ hours. Add water if necessary during cooking to prevent everything from drying out. Longer cooking may be necessary to ensure a tender beef. When serving sprinkle with the chopped parsley.

28th December 1941

A bleak night-crossing in a morose year. / Reverse in North Africa, relentless defeats in the East. / How many ruins have I seen through London, buddleias blooming out of the summer craters, the smell of things, even worse when the weather turns. / This is the lowest point of bitterness, a nation with gritted teeth, *undefeated*. / But no better than that, *undefeated*. / At the Liverpool docks, skinned rabbits and graded butter from Ireland. Censored newspapers. Priests changing out of uniform, becoming a 'Father' once more, shedding the 'Padre.' / And *Movietone News*, land-girls in a Kentish harvest scene, stalemate in the desert. / As we ply the night-boat to Dún Laoghaire. A cup of Horlicks. Three sets of Thomas Wallis cotton sheets for Templemaurice House, ten yards of black-out suède velour for windows that face the Blackwater; £400 certificates in 2½% National War Bonds for safe-keeping. And now, an old Newtown School scholar, limping home from an East London fire-bomb. / Ireland, a poor country? You must be joking, sir. Ireland, never poor, but constantly pillaged. I tell you, when the true history of this land is written it will be an exhaustive list of English and native names. / This neutral land of ours, I tell you, a constant theft. When the great book of Ireland is published, God willing that it won't be in Berlin, I tell you, sir, it will show a continuous theft of the public purse, pensions, confiscations, discoveries, repossessions and plantation, Sweepstakes agents, the well-connected of the Church, you name it, you name the theft. / The Cromwellian Settlement, the inside purchase of Great Southern and Western Shares in 1938. You'd never believe it, Sir, the number who think this land owes them a good living, even in a time of despair. Ah, Ireland. Welcome home. / And I feel the weariness of war, Churchill's voice, quietly fading away.

Arland Ussher's Apricots in Brandy

Mrs. Norah Foley brought this recipe from the kitchens at Lismore Castle. In the 1920s it was a favourite sweet of the writers who came to Templemaurice House as guests of Uncle Walter. Percy Ussher, the young novelist Mrs. Bobby Keane, the dramatist Una Troy, as well as the archaeologist Rev. Dr. Power and the wild young Lady ffrench-McGrath, all partook of that sweet and intoxicating fruit after a noisy dinner of trenchant opinion-sharing.

> 8 fresh apricots, washed, halved and pitted
> ½ cup of water
> Generous ½ cup of brown sugar
> ⅓ cup of brandy
> 2 tablespoons lemon juice
> A thin slice of butter or margarine

Into a heavy casserole put the brandy, lemon juice, water and butter. Combine over a moderate heat for five minutes, allowing the mixture to bubble. Place the apricots, cut side up, in bubbling mixture and cover with the sugar. Cook on stove-top for six or seven minutes, taking care that the syrup is not too reduced. Place in oven to keep warm until serving. For an immediately served dish, place a scoop of vanilla ice-cream at the centre of each plate, place two apricots beside ice-cream and pour warm syrup over.

Dungarvan Bay Crab Preserve

Mrs. Norah Foley cooked all the crab in a big pot, adding half a spoon of salt to every pint of water. Following two or three such meals, Mrs. Foley always preserved the rest of the meat for use as savouries, for picnics or sandwiches. A crab and mayonnaise sandwich was always a favourite treat. Below is the receipt for Mrs. Foley's bottled crab.

> 1 medium crab
> 2-3 ozs of butter
> A sprinkling of anchovy essence
> A little lemon juice
> A hint of cayenne pepper

Chop boiled crab meat finely and pound with a mortar. Mix in two ounces of melted butter, anchovy essence, lemon juice and a hint of cayenne. Mix and then push through a sieve into a cooking jar. Place jar in boiling water and stir until mixture is hot. Turn into small jars. Melt the rest of the butter and pour it over the cooled paste in each little jar. Keep in a cool place.

27th August 1942

The fatigue of old Covenanters still registered in our bones, we attempt a blind date with this new beauty: M4 Sherman, out of Detroit, its 103" width without sandshields, 17" ground clearance, its 83" tread. / Sergeant O'Shea yells in my turret right front, Paax Foley with his assistant in the hull, a quiet lad from Liverpool as loader in the turret, left rear. At speed we try the hydraulic traverse, the 75mm gun and her eight readied rounds. How safe this ammunition seems in its dress of one-inch appliqué armour, welded over the sponson ammunition racks. We glide upon the eight-inch suspension rings, the heavy-duty bogies, earth crushed beneath us at thirteen pounds per square inch. Target at two o'clock, ourselves moving, a lump of crushed metal all yellow and white. O'Shea peers through his direct telescope and roars *Fire!* Boom and recoil, a flash, a blast in the distance, a hit. / And turn, quickly turn, advance, turn, reload at speed, again fire, let loose as well the coaxial machine-guns. Fire, fumes, exhilaration. Eight times this afternoon, not waiting for any piece of metal to cool, with ease and without danger. Not a battlefield, men, not yet. / Four other tank crews try their metal homes, commanders' voices on the radio-net, Irish and Cockney and Liverpool voices; the Micks, a mix. / And later, in the NCOs' Mess, a Sherman party of sorts after the sorting of assessments and reports. / Paax Foley on his Anglo concertina, the Sergeant singing, trying to follow as Paax puts the throttle to the floor. / But Paax beyond him, getting the most power out of his bellows, mastering his air button, lashing through chords, double octaves, triplets and pick-up notes, cross-fingering and legato work. / Paax, the Waterford maestro, all *Harvest Home*, and *Battering Ram* and *Dublin Reel*.

Coolnasmutaun Rowan Jelly

On the Cappoquin road to Mount Melleray through Coolnasmutaun there were many rowan trees or mountain ash growing from the crumbling roadside walls. These berried profusely every summer and autumn, and every autumn without fail Watery Mick Kiely used to bring half a milk churn full of berries to Templemaurice. His reward was always ten shillings and two bottles of the poteen that Mrs. Foley's brother, Mad Jack, used to make.

> 6 lbs of rowan berries
> Water
> Sugar

Wash and drain all berries. Put in a preserving pan and cover with
water. Bring to the boiling point and then simmer slowly until all the
berries look well cooked, soft and broken. Strain through two layers of
muslin tied together or a traditional jelly-bag. Add one pound of sugar
for every pint of liquid. Bring mixture to boiling point and boil rapidly
for ten to fifteen minutes. Test to see if set, pour into a warm container
and fill previously warmed jars. Wait until cool and then cover and
store in a cupboard.

Smaointe Mheadhon Oídhche

Bheadh lucht psychanailíse ag déunamh spóirt le m'óige,
M'athair caillte, lucht na nGearaltach ag fágháil bháis, teanga nach
    maireann;
Caithfidh mé fáithim a chur faoin saoghal san, mo smaointe
Mar ruithleaca na trágha, nó glasóg sa ngiorr-thrághadh.
Thug na Déise cineál mór dhúinn, gnáth-laethanta ag dí-cheangailt
An taidhbhrimh stairiúil. An lá breithe san, 1920 nach mór –
Bád na scannán do tháinig chúm ar taoide na h-Abhann Móire,
Piciúirí *Essanay* mar thaibhsí ar an uisce, m'uncail Walter,
An Ridire Tiarna, na laethanta lán lena phéadóireacht,
Ag déunamh taibhsí gan sceimhleadh dhúinn. Solus Mheiriceá
Ar bhruach na h-abhann, soláidí go leor ar na seolta bána.

Is an t-agallamh Gaoluinne do sgríobh sé dhúinn i n-aimhdheoin
Na nAgallamh Gallda. Chuir an domhan san draíocht ar an saoghal.
Anois i máirseáil tobann na h-oidhche, i n-eagar catha,
Na rian-philéir is tóiteánaigh ós ár gcinn, tagann na gnáth-smaointe
Ag iarraidh foscaidh, saighdiúirí cráite na Guards is Panzer Grenadier
Curtha i n-áirithe ag an stair phráidhneach san, an bás. I m'aigne fhéin,
Bád na sidhe as Eochaill na gCuan, breac-sholus ba bpictiúirí reatha
Ar gach aghaidh neamh-chorthach: Ceapach Chuinn sa gciúineas séimh.

94

Glenshelane Wood Pheasant

Glenshelane Wood, near Cappoquin, Co. Waterford, was old Mrs.
Foley's home turf. There, she had lived in a cottage high in the woods,
from where she could hear the bells of Mount Melleray Abbey while
she sat at her attic window. Only Griffins, O'Donnells, Foleys and
McGraths lived that far up the hill where the Glenafallia and
Glenshelane rivers tumbled downstream each autumn and winter. Mrs.
Foley claims to have caught two hen pheasants with her bare hands
when she was a girl of thirteen or fourteen. She said she hid behind
rowan bushes and waited for the pheasants to pass by on the old Mass
Path that ran through the precipitous end of Glenshelane Wood from
the environs of Belleville House, the home of the novelist Mrs. Keane,
to Mount Melleray Abbey. Hen pheasants, the laziest of God's
creatures, took the line of least resistance and, always on the point of
abandoning their chicks, walked along any path trodden by humans.
Mrs. Foley pounced and caught her prey, wringing their necks. Her
story of that afternoon, an afternoon when she herself was nearly
caught carrying the two pheasants by the artists and flower-gardeners,
the Misses Keane, who lived in the Big House at the end of the wood,
and whose family owned the game rights, that story was always
repeated every time a brace of pheasant was being prepared.
Templemaurice pheasants were always well hung before cooking:
otherwise the flesh would be too dry and firm. The duration of
hanging was always subject to the capriciousness of the West Waterford
weather. If it was warm and humid the hanging process went by
quickly, but in the many sharp, fine cold days of January and February
when pheasant was in season, the process took longer. The pheasant
were always suspended from a rack that hung in the draughty
passageway between the inner stableyard door and the scullery at
Templemaurice. The pheasant was always ready to cook when blood
started dripping from the beak. 'Blood on the beak and it's heavenly,'
Mrs. Foley used to say. If Lady FitzGerald was away and Uncle Walter
was dining Mrs. Foley always placed a piece of beef inside the bird
before cooking. Lady FitzGerald didn't like this, saying that it ruined
the delicate flavours of the fowl.

Brace of pheasant
Half a dozen strips of bacon
Flour
1 oz of dripping

Pluck the bird, singe the skin to get rid of downy feathers. Draw. Wipe inside and out with a wet cloth and then truss firmly. Rub the flour on the bird and lay the bacon slices across the breasts. Heat the dripping in a large roasting tin, or two smaller ones. Place the birds on a grid tray in each tin and cook for an hour. Check after fifty minutes and see if brown and not over-cooking. Reduce the heat if too browned. Place the birds on a dish, having removed the trussing. Pheasant can be served with gravy, watercress, bread sauce or roasted breadcrumbs. Two pheasant should do for six people.

12th November 1942

Once again, the Holyhead ferry / A great pile of civilian clothes in the waiting shed, men poking and pulling, testing the Irish fabric for wear. / This transformation of Englishmen is DeValera's gift to Anthony Eden. Actors in a dressing-room, dressing down for neutrality. / Laughter everywhere, but I remain silent. No stranger will ever know how much this frail neutrality cost / Wars of Independence, a round-up of suspects; 1919, a pistol-whipped poet-teacher in some bogland school / And the ever-open half doors in the light of late morning, letting in the light, keeping out the unwanted. / I think of the hearth gable dug into the slope of rising ground, thatch falling to a Guardsman's height, the annual coat of thickened lime-wash, and the fires that glow best at ground level / Upon a great stone-slab or a cobbled hearth a nation turns to itself for conversation. / I pass through Ireland as a ghost or a carrier of bad luck. And this neutrality like a fire smoored at night by the dutiful housewife, burying what is still alive in the ashes / Bitter experience, Occupation / Only to be fanned once more into a heating blaze, a fire that is a shrine, a half-door for stories that go one way only, fire that warns of weather and wind, of death and ill-luck, of strangers and portents. / And to arrive at Templemaurice in the pure light of early morning / Uncle Walter thumbing through his latest journals, my mother checking again the shelf behind the secret picture-door in the hallway / Once a safe-box for keeping cash and valuables through the Civil War, now a keeper of jams, preserved meats, bottled onions / My mother's secret treasure trove marked *Invasion*.

Villierstown Nettle Soup

Cooking was always associated with reading and writing in Templemaurice House; and in poetry the world created does sometimes have a series of smells, very like a busy kitchen. In the springtime, between early April and mid May, Mrs. Norah Foley served this soup to the entire Templemaurice household in memory of all the people who had died around us in the cabins during the Great Famine. It was always served with the first trout caught in the Finnisk River just below Dromana Bridge. Mrs. Norah Foley would have this soup prepared and ready in the cooler at the beginning of the week when Uncle Walter started fishing in May. She always insisted that it was great for children with measles. But also perfect for adults at war.

> 5 cups of young nettles chopped
> 4 oz of butter
> 1 large leek or 4 spring onion tops chopped
> 1 lb potatoes
> 1½ pints of chicken stock
> Salt and pepper
> Quarter pint of cream is optional, but makes a serving perfect

Heat the butter until it foams. Add the chopped nettles and greens and cook until they look glossy. Stir in the potatoes. Add the stock. Simmer for 30 minutes. Sieve the soup, return to the heat. Add salt and pepper to taste, then the cream cautiously, trying for taste. Too creamy ruins the effect of nettle soup, it is not vichyssoise. Serve really hot. (The above is enough for six people.)

This sauce was once served at a picnic for Princess Alexandra at Lismore Castle at the height of the Edwardian era when Mrs. Foley worked there as a scullery maid – before she came to Templemaurice House as an apprentice cook. When cleaning the plates after the Royal picnic she couldn't resist licking off the sauce when it got onto her fingers. When she asked what the sauce was and then asked for the recipe the cook offered to take her on as an apprentice. From then on her life was a life of contentment in the service of others. 'Food is my salvation, child. May Jesus and His Blessed Mother be praised, my salvation.' And she'd continue her chopping.

2 dessertspoons redcurrant jelly
Quarter pint of port wine
1 tsp of chopped onions
1 tsp of grated orange peel
1 tsp of lemon peel grated
Handful of sultanas
Juice of 1 orange and 1 lemon
A little pepper
A little ginger

Boil chopped peel until tender and strain. Now melt redcurrant jelly and add wine. Add onion and peel and all the other ingredients. Add the sultanas. Simmer all for 15 minutes. Bottle.

Rug an dubh orainn i gCeapach Chuinn

Lampa an stáisiúin ag luascadh anonn is anall i mbior na gaoithe
I gCeapach Chuinn, orgán na traenach ag seinnm ceoil dhúinn.
Mo shaidhbhreas righ na Fódhla, bhí mo mháthair
Faoi dhraíocht ag do chomhrá ar an ardán neodrach –

An oídhche fhliuch san bhíomar sábháilte, dar léi:
Tusa an bhean mhistéireach a thaistealuigheann tré thíortha an
    chogaidh;

Mise a mac gan chosaint air. Bhí sé ina ráfla go raibh
Na mílte marbh thar sáile, ach níor bhaoghal di amharc siar.

Bhí an cogadh iomlán agat, dinnseanchas an Fhaisteachais.
Is gnáth-mhacántacht na bpiléar: an chainnt do gearradh amach go glan
Mar bheannachtaí ar an gcistin neodrach. Bhí cumhacht agat
Orainn, mo stór; is gealach na bpíolótaí an t-ádhbhar machnaimh.

April 4th 1943

Then, quite suddenly, a guard came running along the corridor, shout-
ing 'All blinds down! All blinds down!' / And the air raid sirens of
Paddington / a muffled thumping, the distant percussion of bombs:
bombs falling again on London. / We both reach to pull the blinds. 'Tell
me about the poems,' she says. *Tuar guil, a cholaim, do cheól!* A poet cries
from Professor O'Rahilly's *Measgra Dánta*. / And I begin to tell her
about the lost Gaelic world far away from this war outside the windows
of the railway carriage. Our train comes to a halt. / Shudder. It starts to
move again. She peers through the blind. 'A bomb has started a fire,' she
said, 'there's smoke billowing from that building.' The train halts again.
More sounds of falling bombs. / A sound of steam being released, a train
shunting beside us, backing up on the line. 'It's empty, the train' she
whispered. All the windows are shattered. It must have been caught by
the blast.' She takes my hand in her very fine hands, well-bred hands.
'Will you say those strange words again.' / And I recite the Irish words,
this time full of emotion. A kind of silence folds about us / silence
outside, a silence that seems to last for days in the darkened carriage. We
move again. The platform. Her destination. The 'All Clear' sounds. /
When we get down from the carriage I am not sure of the next move. A
glass roof has been blown in / the waiting room near us is a mess of dust
and glass and shattered brick. Who will send a Captain Kirwan to rebuild
our poems? ARP wardens in tin helmets come running along the plat-
form, inspecting the damage. 'Do come to my place, my rooms are
nearby,' she said. 'Have a shot of Scotch. I've nothing Irish. / Stay
awhile, stay.'

Lady FitzGerald loved Dinny Mescall, who ran the grocery shop and
dairy store at the Square in Cappoquin. She loved the shop especially
on Sunday mornings and travelled into Cappoquin for no other reason
than to be part of the throng of after-Mass women who waited in line
to be served personally by Dinny. Dinny was a favourite at
Templemaurice House because he sold Mrs. Foley's surplus
Tallowbridge Fudge and sold the excess lettuces, cabbages and
strawberries from the garden. The income from these sales was split
evenly between my mother and Mrs. Foley (Mrs. Foley was due
income because she organized the picking and pulling and boxing and
it was *her* kitchen and *her* economy that allowed such excessive
production to accumulate in the garden). May Cassidy ran a shop in
Barrack Street and had a fine stand of gooseberries in the wild garden
that ran between the back of her shop and the wall of Sir John Keane's
estate. May sold her bottled gooseberry sauce to a selected clientele,
never offering it for sale to the residents of Barrack Street and the
Nuns' Houses across the road; people she considered (unfairly) a
low-born ex-garrison rabble.

    1 freshly caught mackerel per person
    Salt, pepper, teaspoon of mustard
    2 oz margarine

a. *The mackerel*

Remove head and trim fins and tail. Make a small knife cut on the
underside of the fish and remove guts and roe. Rub insides with salt.
Wash and dry fish (to prevent scorching). Make a mixture of salt,
pepper, mustard and a little melted margarine (or oil). Brush the fish
well with his mixture. Replace the roe. Place the fish on a greased grid.
Grill for three minutes, turn and grill three minutes, turn again, grill,
turn again, grill. Serve on a dish with either a caper sauce or with

b. *Gooseberry sauce*

Half pint of gooseberries
1 oz melted butter
A little flour
1 tsp caster sugar
Pinch of nutmeg

Top and tail gooseberries. Stew in water until soft, just enough water
to prevent burning. Rub through a fine sieve. Take one desertspoon of
flour and the melted butter and blend; cook together for ten minutes,
stirring. Add this thickening to the gooseberry pulp. Heat together for
about thirty minutes with the sugar and pinch of nutmeg. Serve hot
with the mackerel.

Dromana House Lime Marmalade

This was Uncle Walter's absolutely favourite taste, a marmalade that
was frequently made at a neighbouring mansion on the hill, historic
Dromana House. Uncle always kept his lime jam in the muslin-draped
cooler in the stable yard. A June/July alfresco tea that he took down by
the boathouse, with his books on his lap and his two black Labradors
by his side – one could see him from the upper verandah or while
running down the steps to the river. I carry that image of my Uncle
Walter as a timeless and immortal image of all Irish childhoods.

4 lb limes
1 lb sweet oranges
Sugar
8 pints of water

Cut fruit in two and remove pips. Drop pips into a basin with quarter
pint of warm water. Cover and leave in warm place. Squeeze the juice
from fruit and place in a pan. Mince the remainder of the fruit and add
the juice to the water. Cover and stand overnight. Next day, add the
liquid from the pips in the basin and simmer the lot until the fruit is

tender. Measure all, and add one pound of sugar for every pint of liquid. Bring to the boil and boil rapidly (keep watching) until a set is made. This usually takes fifteen minutes. Pour off into a warmed container and fill warm jars. When cooled cover and store.

20th May 1943

Putting aside the February edition of the Dublin *Bell*, I quote its essay on Gaelic: 'The Gaeltacht, the language, the Revival, everything associated with what was once so honoured and so nourishing, is now a bitter taste in the mouth, sometimes positively nauseating.' That's the message from Ireland, that and the brave O'Donnell essay *Cry Jew!* But your hand like an altar-boy's paten is placed beneath the cigarette's long ash. You make it to the brass ash-tray, a *Souvenir of Brighton* from 1936. The ash drops and you pull again, deep and anxious and grateful: a cigarette. I laugh at your need and you scoff at my lack of need for cigarettes / At which I take an ancient Dutch cigar from its silver submarine capsule, trim and light up with a blazing spill of paper. Puff into your face. Coughing laughter. / It is intimate, your three London rooms, intimate and hermetic, like a small neutral country / We have made this place to come to, how bizarre. Not a place, as such, but a series of events growing ever exclusive, concerning only us. It is too intense and immediate. I think like this. But then so is the whole of London, full now only of necessary, licensed people. / Schoolmates burned to death and last year's collision of the *Curaçao* and the *Queen Mary* off Donegal / Chance, not war, our numbers coming up. Must come up / Ah, ash, cigar smoke, music / Me in my uniform and you still with your civilian Russian hero look, a winter coat in late May, a bed to sleep in, you say, nearly half your clothing coupons gone in one Selfridges afternoon / Why you eschew your Captain's uniform you will not tell, not yet / Your office work, cigarette smoke, lover's fatigue, all fold within a single consciousness, an undeclared purpose / I know it well, your delayed goodbye.

Mionteagasc roimh chath 1944

An gairdín a bhí againn sna Déisibh uair amhain sa domhan eile –

Órshúlach lus an chromchinn gach Máirt;
Sa Bhealtaine, páipéirí bán-dearga bláthanna na n-ubhall,
Craobhacha dorcha na bhfigí úra 's muid ag déunamh folachán;
An teach-gloine 'bhí monartha i bPaisley na hAlban;

Na fionchaora saidhbhreach fé smacht lách mo mháthar,
An torthóir draíochtúil i gCois Móire Cois Bríde –
Is teanga phearsanta ag gach duine ar aonach an Déardaoin
I gCeapach Chuinn, teanga nach mbeidh san Eoraip dhóite arís;

Comhluadar Chois Móire, canamhain bhinn na nDéise.
Feicim m'óige tré fhuinneúgaibh smúideamhala an chogaidh;
Airtléire is tancanna a chuireann droch-cháil ar gach máthair,
Í loiscthe in a beathaidh, a tigh i n-aon chaorthainn amháin,

'Gus tíortha nach maireann; cheapas, tráth, go mbeidís ann go deo,
Anso i gceartlár an *bocage* roimh 'Ordú Gluaiseachta'
Chím ubhall-ghort Normandy, 'cuimhin liom Baile Nua is Ceapach
  Chuinn;
Fuinniúga briste na filídheachta, Árus Templemaurice ar m'amharc.

March 12th 1944

Came the bright candle of Máirtín Ó Díreáin, a Gaelic certainty of being from an Aran Island; poems more sympathetic and free than Arland Ussher, dear Percy in his falling-down Cappagh House, or Uncle Walter could ever dream of in their Déise lore. / We watch Louis Jouvet and Suzy Prim in *The Heart of a Nation*. Our stolen afternoon at The Academy in Oxford Street. / Now hopeful as an island candle burning in Ó Díreáin, chastened in the College at Camberley, I lectured to fresh-faced cadets on *Standing Orders of the Brigade of Guards* and preparations for war. / Ó Díreáin's Irish poetry was a kind of consecrated Host as I walked corridors in a Kingdom that now held its breath on behalf of every poet who was free to breathe. / Even those, let it be said in verse, who held to that Celtic belief in remaining neutral, peripheral, in a time of grief. Yet this book came as a gift from Uncle Walter, I in mufti in Jammets, my uncle greedily at work upon his pudding. He had met the new poet on a Galway train, Connaught Irish and Déise Irish the sudden bond between them. / How unreal the world is to us of the Celtic fringe, how unreal the war seemed to anyone out fly-fishing, watching the Corrib unfold. / And yet Dublin was alive that summer, alive with a peculiar, compressed being. If it was neutrality it was a creative thing, yet creative mainly for the detritus, the flotsam of war, that floated into Dublin Bay from the world in conflict not far away. / How consoling the courtesies of neutrality seem, how courteous the women of a western island. / An ocean without submarines swelled through Ó Díreáin's phrases, the wind whistled through the dry-stone rigging of such poems.

Oidhche roimh chath, 1944

Bhí suaimhneas éigint le fáil againn sna laethanta samhraidh san;
Sean-oidhreacht na sinsear, conách gleoidhte na ngaolta;
Mise, mar shicín tradhna, ag ruith tré phleascanna cruithneachta
Cois Abha Mhór na nDéise ag canadh 'Máthair! Máthair!'
Gach nóta maighdeanúil, gan cuirpeacht na mblianta –

Urnuighthe na síolrach sa bhruidhean cois abhann; sgléip
An tsamhraidh ar gach rud sa dtalamh freagarthach, sa ngairdín
     meadhrach.
Cloisim an fonn neamhchoitianta san oidhche roimh chath,
An mhórchuid saidhbhris curtha i dtaisce agam, ceol
Mo mhuinntire. Ní dóigh liom gur thug aoinne an ceol ceart uainn.

Saghdiúirí Black Watch

Saighdiúirí tuirseach ag teacht chun tosaigh,
Croíléiseach an dream iad ag gabháil *spin*
As gach tanc na Micks i mbreacadh an lae.
Na h-Oifigigh sinnsir ag siúl go tapaidh,
Iad ag dul ar seachrán céille, trioslóg ar thrioslóg,
Ag béicigh i nGaoluinn na h-Alban –

An Teanga mar chosaint orthu, is beannacht.

Déshúiligh Bhriste 1944

Deoir fhearthainne ar mo dhéshúilibh mar dheoir dheireanach
Na Mór-Roinne traochta; an ciúineas tar éis fhiabhras an chatha
Ar gach rud ar talamh; tosnuighim ag sgríobh
Ar pháipéar buí an HMSO. Thá boladh toite ar gach
Smaoineamh, an boladh ar gach rud ó chóngas gunnaí 88mm.

'Cuimhin liom an siuc thar oidhche is an sneachta i gCnoc Meilleirí,
Boladh toite an gheimhridh, sneachta chomh mion le gaineamh na
     hEochaille,
Duine eicínt ag gleo; buidéal dubh ar an dubhadán,
An fhilidheacht á gearradh amach go glan, mo línte cortha den
     chogadh.

Anocht, eascruigheann an sneachta as an bháisteach stairiúil,
Brón agus briseadh croidhe, smál dubhaigh ar an stair –
Tagann mo dhán úr leis na saighdiúirí gortuighthe; mo shúile
Ar na nithibh nach féidir a mhúineadh; bás, féile is filidheacht.

Póca Falaise, 1944

Na Micks anso gan paidir a rá; cuirim ar a súilibh dóibh,
Muid go léir spíonta amach sa choill bhig;
Bocage an Ifrinn, an talamh ag gearán go géar;
Saighdiúirí ag tarraingt an chupán tae, iad caochta leis an ocras –
Mé féin ag faire sa marbhán samhraidh;
Ruainne síothchána againn, dán agam dom héinnigh.

Thá siad thíos ansan i dtóchar leathan
A srónta iarainn, an bás acu mar neantóg cholgach,
Mathghamhain liath an tanc-Tiger. Ní de threibh Dhann-Garbhán iad,
Is amhla a sgríos an dán so ach imtheacht i ndiaidh mo chinn;
Bocage an scannar-bhuaidhreadh,
'gus na Micks anso ar fhaonfhleasc a ndroma –
an sceimhleadh á aistriughadh ó theangain go teangain.

July 17th 1944

A briefing at Divisional Command before the move. / Vimonte. A Waterford garden comes through the dust, a dream to overwhelm me, visions from another world. The golden syrup of daffodils, every March in bloom, and May the pink paper-blossom of apple trees, the dark branches of our fig tree as we play hide-and-seek / A palatial greenhouse built in Paisley, Scotland / Rich grapes under my mother's discipline, the magical fruit-gardener of Waterford / And the language? That personal language with everyone and everything on a Thursday's Fair-Day in Cappoquin, a language never again seen in burning Europe / Companionship of the Blackwater, sweet conversation of the Decies. / Childhood visits us through the misted glass of battle, artillery and tanks bring disgrace upon everything maternal. / Nations that no longer live. / How, before each battle-briefing, we think that things might live forever. Here in the *bocage*, before the Movement Order, we see only the orchards of Normandy. / I remember somehow, remember in this noise Villierstown and Cappoquin / Broken windows of poetry / Temple-maurice in my sights. / Midnight and another agitated wait before the move. Like a madman in some film of the pre-War years, I pace the narrow aisle between tanks and half-tracks. / And I think, how the psycho-analyst must view this creature in the dark. A father lost long ago, Geraldines of the South swiftly passing away. A birthday long ago in the 1920s, Uncle Walter full of mischief-making, writing Irish words for the *Essanay* dialogue. / Here beside me, terror, tracer-bullets, Guards and Panzer Grenadiers reserved by the urgent greed of history. Pacing the analytic night, flickering light of cinema upon our children's faces. Cappoquin in the sublime quiet. / Attack by 1-2C, crossing the bridge at Orne. / Cagney averted, Cagney averted. / And Cappoquin never forgotten.

Mount Melleray Colcannon and Champagne

This was what Paax Foley missed as he rushed away from Ireland and his mother's Templemaurice cooking. Uncle Walter always insisted on this meal on the great night of the Celts, Hallowe'en. He reminded them of the name, 'cal ceann fhionn', literally 'white headed cabbage.' It is traditionally made from chopped kale or white cabbage. At Templemaurice House the colcannon contained a ring, a shilling, a button and a silver thimble. The one who found the ring would be married by next Hallowe'en, the shilling meant a life of wealth, the thimble meant spinsterhood and the button bachelorhood. Uncle Walter always gave Clonmel cider to the children instead of champagne.

> 1 lb kale or white cabbage
> 1 lb potatoes
> 2 small leeks or green onion stems
> Quarter pint of milk
> Salt and pepper
> A few drops of Worcester sauce
> 4 ounces butter

Cook kale / cabbage in boiling water until tender. Don't overcook. Drain and chop finely. Cook potatoes. Chop leeks or onion and simmer in milk for 10 minutes. Drain potatoes, season, mash well, then stir in leeks and milk. Stir in the finely chopped kale. Make well in centre of mixture and put in the butter. Heat and mix entire in a heavy frying pan and keep heating until a light crust is formed. Turn out onto a large plate and keep hot. If you come from a Celtic nation, serve with NV champagne or Asti Spumante. Otherwise, serve with a good English cider.

August 11th, 1944

Onward we plunge. Fumes and dust and heat / Shudder and trundle of the heavy Sherman as she labours onward / Relentless chatter, far away and intimate, squadron, brigade, H.Q., never soothing. Eyes terrified and alert. *Psssssssh Shhhhhhhmmmmhhhh.* Like a bicycle tyre slowly deflating, a dying commander is expelled into his microphone. A corpse attached to the comms. system. Everyone knows. / Dread. Death. Dread. Onward we plunge and plunge. Onward. A crash, a flame, another hit. All of us will die here. The battalion will be wiped out, armour and marching companies. Petrol fumes, death / Stop. Reverse. Forward. Traverse. Tail-lights of the lead tank in a swirling dust. Suffocation. Dust. Wrong squadron. Damn. Driver. Damn. Halt. The net. Noise. Roaring command. All bathe in the roar, the rage, more flashes of light. Flames. Tank of another squadron is hit, leading the wrong squad. Explosions of auxiliary tanks and shells, fireworks in the darkened mid-summer afternoon. / And then an end to it. / An evening. / The hatch opening, fresh air, dust. / Something that blew in the wind has snaffled on the hatch. A long strip of parachute silk, long as a picnic cloth laid upon the river field at Cappoquin. Silk out of the sand and dust of the roads, suffocating roads. / Eyes and mouth moulded by sandpaper. / I stretch for the silk, long parted from its para-trooper, grab until it comes away, cool and smooth as if waiting to be received. I stretch it, fold it, roll it, cool silk over my mouth and nose. The air is cold through it, like home. / In this way begins the poem.

Ar an mBóthar go Nijmegen, 1944

Beirim greim ar lámha fuaraigeanta na filidheachta.
Anois thá an bhuamáil ag dul in olcas,
Scréach an Typhoon idir an bhóthar is an spéir;
An droichead nimhneach fé phleancadh.
Thá ár bpíolóta fé gheasaibh ag na ribíní buí,
Muid go léir ag feitheamh fén gcomh-aontas geal.

Thíos an bóthar thá na Gearmánaigh i bhfolach –
Panzer Grenadiers, saighdiúirí oilte an Oirthir.
Thá foireann an tanc so ar bior an scanraidh,
Gach fear ag feitheamh. Briseann scáird-eitleán
Ós ár gcinn, milliún síol oráiste
Scaipthe, ag druidim anuas go tapaidh.
Buachaill óg, a dheora tráighte
'Guardsman!' a deirim, 'Guardsman Ó Faoláin,
An cuimhin leat an oidhche san, 1938, ár Jack Doyle –

Nach raibh na sluaighte ann is Jack is canadh?
Sár-dornálaí na Micks, blas Kilburn agus Hollywood san aer;
Ní raibh Jack faoi sceimhleadh an oidhche san
Ach é ag canadh, ag snámh i n-aghaidh easa,
Is ag cainnt faoi mhná Chearnóg Sloane.
Éist leis an gceol, a bhuachaill, as an bhearna baoghail.

Luibh na Seacht nGábhadh, 1944

Teas agus smút agus scread na Sherman corruighthe:
Téighimid ar aghaidh go dtí Villiers Bocage,
An bealach oscailte againn ar pháirc an Áir;
Sáirsint ar an líon-radio ag cur faitchis ar gach aoinne,
An gunnadóir as an Aird Mhór ag canadh 'Galway Bay'.
Cuimhin liom An Cosáinín, an Chúilín Mhuire, Luibh
A' Treatha, Luibh na n-Aosán is an Feochadán Fiadh –

Agus Luibh na Seacht nGábhadh; ainmneacha áitiúla
Na nDéise as béul m'uncail Walter: leigheas draíochta
Don tiománaí gortuighthe, creabh-dhearg,
É gaiste anois san tanc a dh'iompuigh ar a bhéul fé;
Fuar-allas an sceoin orainn – muid i dtaca leis an gclaidhe.

August 14th 1944

A mile behind us the Scots in their Churchills of the 6th Guards, heavy shell and mortar-fire, inadequate infantry cover to hold a ridge. / Ambushed in the dust by a unit of the Waffen SS, we scramble, retreat, flare out, regroup, attack, drive like a donkey with his arse on fire into a harbour of metal and 88mms. / And then, suddenly, abruptly after contact, the enemy withdrawing, dust settling. Eerie silence as engines are cut. Paax Foley starting up a quick brew, ah, tea, a few Woodbines from home: a quick pee, emptying of urine tins. / Our first jettison tank suspended from a tree. RAF Sgt Pat Barron's hand-writing in signal-box red, with a Greek inscription: *Welcome, Heroes*. Ah, dat's Pat. He learned his Greek from the Augustinians in Dungarvan. Dat's Pat alright. / *Fokine* hell, we're in Pat's drop zone! / What drop-zone? / Guinness, Jameson, Drink. That's our drink hangin' from da trees! We must move on, Sir! Some other regiment might take our drink! / *I must talk to the Colonel. Must speak with Brigade H.Q.* / 'Tis da Canadians on our left, they've gone ahead. Dey have our Guinness! *Mudderajasus* / Leaving Terence O'Neill to play with his pet Mongol, we run ahead with our Firefly, the 176th tank that the 2nd Battalion never lost. / And there, in an orchard, filled with a stench of decomposing cows, we find a fiery Canadian coven of parachutists / And we get our gifts of Guinness from James Gate, metal-wrapped, tubular, with thirty per cent to our heroic Canadian friends. After which we dine together, the Colonel and I, on one small tin of Beluga caviar from Fortnum and Mason, my last luxury, and a full litre of the best Leoville preserved for weeks in a greased binocular-case. Caviar. Broken binoculars. Colonel Kleinzahler of Toronto. *Déinigi annlan anis den a bhfuil agaibh. Sir, things could be worse*, Corporal Foley opines, mess-tin in hand, walking sideways.

Sir John Keane's Summer Pudding

My Uncle Walter and Senator Sir John Keane were the best of friends, joking, bartering, gossiping (mainly about Lord Longford's and Percy Ussher's personal life and the actresses of the Gate Theatre). Sir John often brought a gallon of blackberries to our kitchen in the autumn before he returned to his work in the Irish Senate or at the Bank of Ireland in Dublin. These blackberries were the main ingredients of his Summer Pudding. It is also a fact that the pudding was made by Mrs. Foley more often in late September when blackberries and sweet apples were plentiful.

½ pound blackberries or blackcurrants
6 ounces of sugar
½ pound raspberries or red berries
Slices of white bread, thinly cut
2 good apples cut into small pieces
¼ pint of water

Clean fruit, removing stalks and peel and chop apples. Place water and sugar in saucepan and heat until sugar dissolves, then add the fruit. Remove the crusts from sliced bread and line the soufflé dish or bowl. Fill the mould with the simmered fruit. Cover completely with more bread slices and place a weight on top. Chill in a refrigerator, preferably overnight. To serve, up-end the bowl onto another dish to release the mould of summer pudding. Best served with cream, but not excessive amounts of cream, as the musty fruitiness of this pudding is its own reward.

April 4th 1945

Evening attack at HAMB / Shells rain upon us / So much for a defeated Germany, the enemy fights and fights and fights / Sixty casualties / A night attack across the woods, a 3rd Battalion diversionary attack goes well, two companies sweeping across the hill / A fatal dawn attack, Michael Dudley killed / This late in the war, such bitterness among friends, Michael following Brian Russell to his German grave / Determined, we move on, move on; taking fewer prisoners, becoming hardened / Find a safe harbour, liberate a limousine from a Schloss, begin to plan again fine wine and dining in Brussels with Will Berridge and Desmond Fitz. / Until, *damn, shit* / A hit / A sniper catches me in the upper arm. / To the dressing station where the wound is cleaned, an affable American slumming with the Micks, cleaning, disinfectant that stings and stings, a surgeon dismissing me as nothing much. Press hard upon it and keep it there / From behind a curtain, screams 'It can't breathe! It can't breathe! It's punctured, Christ Almighty! Ye'll have to do something, / Paax Foley's familiar tones. Paax in trouble / Well / A young surgeon checks the extended bellows of an Anglo concertina, another sniper casualty. I'll use a piece of skin-tissue to cover that, Paax. Thanks, Sir. / And gets to work, sewing and sealing, bringing the notes back, breath by breath / Then an injured soldier hobbles in, bleeding, injury at a bridge, an unexploded ordnance / He'll have to wait, I'm trying to seal Paax Foley's organ / And wait he does, bleeding, in pain, a nod of acknowledgement to all the company, blood streaming from his shrapnel wound / A cigarette, anyone?

Mrs. Foley's Brown Soda Bread

Mrs. Norah Foley always made four loaves of soda bread at a time. The making of bread was always accompanied by some ceremony and speech-making: the clearing and scrubbing of the table, the expression of melancholy thoughts about the Great Famine, especially Mrs. Foley's story of the murder of starving poor people in Dungarvan who tried to get at a grain-store. 'Ah, bread is what bates us women down,' Mrs. Foley used to say, 'bates us down, child. Ye men goes off to war and goes off to ye're horses and da poor women are left in the kitchen bakin da bread. Madame Maud Gonne was right when she spoke at the Land League, dis life is never fair, neither to the murdered poor of Dungarvan nor to da women of Ireland.' One day Paax Foley made the grave mistake of telling his mother that while her bread was good it wasn't nearly as good as Mrs. Barron's bread in Cappoquin. One hot loaf was flung across the kitchen, breaking against his indiscreet head:

'If I had the lovely brick ovens that Barrons in Cappoquin have,
instead of this broken-down old range, I'd make your perfect loaf too.
You ungrateful pup!' Paax's opinion notwithstanding, Mrs. Foley
produced a mighty loaf of bread. Here's the recipe.

Three cups of wholemeal flour
Two cups of bran
1 tsp salt
1 tsp bread soda
Sour milk

Mix all the ingredients together to form a stiff dough, taking care not
to use too much milk. Knead well, flatten to about two inches in
thickness. Cut a deep gash in the middle with a knife, brush with the
milk and bake in a fairly hot oven until it makes a hollow sound when
the bottom is tapped.

Mí an Aibreáin san Ollchampa Géibhinn, 1945

Codladh corrach againn; an stair i gcliabhán dorcha:
Campa géibhinn do phríosúnaigh phoilitidheachta, na sean-fhir mar
    thaibhsí
As an Droch-Shaoghal, tocht guil tagtha orthu.
An Aibreán is nimhnighe riamh: muid ag féuchaint
Ar lámh-cheird na h-Eorpa. A Íosa, Íobairt Dhóighte!
Isteach linn sa gcliabhán nimhneach Sandbostel;
Filí is cumadóirí na Fraince curtha isteach i gcás,
Tuth an mhorgaidh, boladh an Fhaisisteachais.

Na saighdiúirí SS ag béicigh 'Nicht Nazi, Nicht Nazi'.

Níl aon bhuadh le fágháil anso, tada ar bith don gnáth-shaighdiúir –
An príosún so ag seoladh mar bhád iascaigh
As Heilvick, ag druidim faoi sholus na gealaighe,
Scréachóg roilige ag cur ceisteanna orainn:
Cad athá anso san uaigneas? –

Nil anso ach corp nochtuighthe na h-oidhche,
Na crainn sínte ar ardtalamh mar speitheánach sa bhFeabhra.

'Cad a tharla anso, a Ghearalaigh?'
Éigse na ndraoithe, dréacht-ghlan, im chroí,
Dólás an domhain im' intinn.
Cloisim fuar-chaoineadh coscrach na bpríosúnach.
Smaoinighim ar fhaisistíoch na neodrachta, lucht an tír-ghrádha
'gus an tonn-taoscacht tagtha orthu i dtithe tábhairne i nÉirinn;
Púdar-gunna na staire ag deargadh ina gcomhluadar;
Is follasach nár dhein an Cogadh mórán imnidhe dóibh
Smaoinighim ar an gcroich athá im thaobh
I n-áit mo dhoilghis díomhaoin: agus, sa lá ag diúltughadh dá sholas

Gach máthair Eorpach, ainniseach mar chearc fhraoich, ag tónacáil
    uainn
Lena Críost pearsannta; a chuid éadaigh millte 'ge luairtheán a'
    bhóthair.

An Ceannaire Foley i gCampa Sandbostel, 1945

Saoghal fada le séun chughat, a cheannaire Foley,
As ucht an chrógacht do bhí le feiscint againn
Sa *bocage* malluighthe. 'Cuimhin liom do mháthair chráite
Ag fanacht leat i mbothán na h-iascaireachta –
Tigh beag leis na fuinneúgaibh briste:
Sciúirseáil fearthainne na nDéise ag bagairt uirthi:
Í sceimhlighthe le h-eagla go mbainfeadh dada duit –
Ach fuair tú an ceannsmacht orthu go léir:
Gach soiscéal craobh-scaoilte agat tar éis magh an Áir.

Tháimid ó bhaoghal anois, sinn na fir mhór-sgéulta 'gus seanchuis;
Seaghan Mac Séamais agat, corn fíona dhá dhiúghadh agam;
Ach is cuimhin liom an lá san san Ollchampa,
Aidhbhle d'eolchaire tar éis an choinghleic chalma;

An garda SS a bhí g-eite ar chuma éigint ar a chois.
É ar meisce, ag gáire fút. Thug tú fobha féigh,
Deora na nDéise ar d'aghaidh, aghaidh a smearaigh
An cogadh. Bhí cruálacht an Fhaisisteachais tharat;
– Éagóir na poilitidheachta cladhartha, daoine dalla –

An náisiún príobháideach do dheineamar
Fé éide Ghallda: saol ionraic san Íodhbairt Dhóite.

April 29th 1945

Flesh. / Smoke. / History nests in this dark cage of Europe; prison-camp of political prisoners: such women, ghosts from the Great Famine, the black potatoes of their broken hearts. The most poisonous springtime ever, us looking at the handiwork of Europe. / Dear Christ, a Holocaust. / In we go, Irish and Grenadier, into the poisoned cage of Sandbostel: poets and philosophers of France under lock and key, scent of death, taste of Fascism. Prison guards shouting 'Nicht Nazi! Nicht Nazi!' The SS heroes already run away. Guardsmen! Let me cut a poem in stone: for Kenneally and Charleton, for the others who lost their lives between desert and sea, between bridge and canal and flooded Dutch towns; for those Irishmen with shattered arms, holding their Brownings against their dying frames. / But there's no victory here, nothing left for the ordinary Irish Guardsman. / This prison sails across history like the fishing boat out of neutral Helvick, slipping away under the light of the moon. The screech-owl questions us: what happened here in this lonely place? Nothing here but the naked body of the night, the trees stretched on a hillock like dead soldiers. / 'What happened here, Oh, Geraldine?' / Poetry of desperation in my heart, sadness of this earth in my mind. I hear prisoners screaming / the gun-powder of history red with blood. I think of the grief around me instead of liberation. Every wretched mother of Europe, like a hen pheasant in the woods at Glenshelane, stealing away with her own personal Christ; her last possible Christ in this ruin / this ruin of Europe's soul.

Mr. Redmond's Fingers

This is the name Mrs. Foley gave to a very simple sandwich, cut into thin slices or 'fingers.' The ingredients are very basic:

Sliced white or brown bread
Half pound of cooked chicken breast
Quarter pound of ham
2 tablespoons of grated cheese
3 yolks of eggs, hard-boiled
Salt, pepper, a dash of vinegar, a sprinkle of mustard
Olive oil, enough to moisten the mixture

Chop all the ham and the chicken very finely and mix them thoroughly, pounding in a mortar, if available, or in a bowl, with the egg yolks and the grated cheese. Add the salt, pepper, mustard and vinegar to the mixture. Only add as much olive oil as required to moisten the filling. Butter the thinly sliced bread and spread the mixture over half the slices. Cover with the other slices and then cut neatly into narrow fingers or triangles. Mrs. Foley always said that these fingers, in large enough quantities, were more than enough to satisfy any reception that was overwhelmingly male. If women were going to be present, reception food was always more problematic and challenging. For women, Mrs. Foley always prepared a variety of shaped 'fingers' filled with salmon, anchovy, caviar and cayenne or foie gras; all of these neatly placed on folded paper napkins and then placed on linen-covered silver platters. 'In any public gathering,' Mrs. Foley was fond of saying, 'men are easily fooled. But in the same situation women are even more cranky and alert.'

1st May 1945

Grim the faces of French officials, liaison officers, nurses and philosophers / Silent the victims, the Holocaust turns its graceful face to us / Fascism presents its disgraceful face to a German spring / Who would deny it all now? Who could deny this, before our eyes, the Fascists' unforgivable handiwork. / Ambulances, canvas-covered lorries, jeeps, even a half-track that was used to demolish a lattice-work wall, all, all, all called into service, four miles to the main railway-station, the long train journey back to hospitals in France. / At this gate we complete our honest journey, in a uniform not of our own nation. But a Regiment of our own. / A fresh poem in my satchel, another poem about war in a resolutely neutral tongue: Ye'll be galloping back, I suppose, *ag filleadh ar cosa in airde*, Uncle Walter writes. / As if it mattered now, any sense of triumph. / Too late / I read Mr. Gogán's haunting line from his poem in *Comhar*: *Tá an traein ag feitheamhh is an t-inneall go tréan i dtúin* and Mr. Ó Céileachair's *Ó imthighis uainn a ghrádh, do thréaig an ghrian an lá* and wonder at the trains of Europe that has bled so many mothers and lovers dry / Such a luxury of language in a place like this, a stench of Sandbostel / And the helping over, the carrying. Paax Foley and his four Micks start a brew-up by the mud-caked wheels of a half-track. / A job done, a death-camp emptied. / No one coming forward to accept shame. No one, exquisite choreography of denial / I correct my little poem while Paax – opinionated, enraged, yapping 'Glad we made it to here, Sir. Glad I came back to the Regiment in '19 and '39.' – takes his healed concertina and lashes into a march of reels, jigs and hornpipes / *The Mason's Apron, The Lark in the Clear Air, The Cuckoo's Nest.*

Oidhche na Nollag sa Bhruiséil, 1945

I

Seacláid spleodrach is branda is branda ólta againn
Tar éis an chóisir meadhon oidhche; níl aon snáithe ort
Ar na comhlaí infhillte, tú ag caint le Dónal na gealaighe.
Thá na fuinneoga oscailte os comhair 'Eye Club' na Guards;
Ceol rinnce Meiriceánach ag borradh agus ag caolughadh.
Téigheann tú nochtaithe anocht sa mBruiséil fuascailte,
Airgead sholas na gealaighe an dath tathagach 'nois –
Níl an oidhche fúinn fhéin, a stór, thá na ragaiméalaí
Ag briollacadh ort ag deireadh na cóisire:

Cuireann tú maise ar fhlúirse na Nodlag.
Léirigh ort go mear! Thá na sluaite as Cór XXX,
Saighdiúirí sólásacha an Mharcshlua Ríoga i ngrádh leat,
Cnú mo chroídhe, grá na h-oidhche, beidh na milseáin á n-diúl againn.

2

Thá d'fholt glórmhar níos doinne, níos donn-deirge ar fad,
Is í trilseach, ach cosúil le sneachta sa Ghearmáin
Timpeall do chluasa. Cuirim póg is póg,
Is póg eile, ar do mhuc shneachta, cóta an t-sionnaigh –
Chomh líonrach leis an Rhine sa bhFóghmhar;
Chomh h-aoibhinn leis an saighdiúir Eorpach ar meisce.

3

An fear céile athá caillte agat, an tAimiréal i gClub na hOidhche
Measaim nach gcreidfeadh sé an t-uafás
Athá beirthe againn, bréalacán an ghrádha.
'A stór', deireann tú go práidhneach 'beidh mé id' bhean-chéile.'

Raibh an grádh ag cur ciméara orainn? Cinnte, cinnte.

16th June 1945

No word of her for weeks and weeks, no letters in the post, no cards, no
telegram / No word left at the Eye Club in Brussels, no word left with
Giles in the Brigade or Desmond Brownlow in Divisional H.Q. / No
word between the political camp inspections and our arrival in Cologne.
/ Such an emptiness and anti-climax. / Quite suddenly I am full of
hatred, stress of waiting, gate-fever, as our love walks the corridor of the
condemned. / It is Europe. Get used to the idea of loss / Cologne in
pieces, its very soul shattered. / Until now, walking disconsolately in a
victor's uniform, I fall upon an English book, lying perfectly clean and
undamaged, on a mangled park bench: William Rothenstein's *Men and
Memories*, published by Faber in a long-lost era of innocence. / I look

around. It has no owner. It is an orphaned book in a shattered landscape. / There, the 1890s of lady water-colourists, colouring the coast between Rapallo and Spezia, preparing the soul for a Goupil Gallery retrospective, cool interiors of Hampstead, fluent Cotswold portraits / Rubble beneath my feet, exhausted women carting bricks in children's prams / I carry a piece of my mother's England as rare now as a Gaelic island, as holy and lovely. Roger Fry praises this world. Havelock Ellis sits / No word from her these dreadful weeks. The world grown serious as a pastel of Conrad on brown paper, world as desolate and silent as the ruined *Church at Bourlon, 1918* / To Ellen Terry he wrote 'Miss Terry, my nights have been sleepless – my drawing sitting gibbering on my chest' / What a treasure to find on a mangled Cologne bench / Just one card from her would do. One card. A signature.

Mick Sargent's Cappoquin Bacon and Savoy Cabbage

> 4–5 lbs of good bacon
> Three onions
> Water
> A Savoy cabbage, heart quartered. Outer leaves chopped.

Affable, kindly, big-hearted and witty, Michael Sargent was one of the most popular businessmen of West Waterford. For decades he was proprietor of Sargent's Garage, one of Cappoquin's most visible and successful businesses. All of the Templemaurice cars were serviced at Sargent's over the years. My mother and Mick were great *connoisseurs* of bacon and bacon curing. They were both proud of the produce of Robert Keane's Cappoquin Bacon Factory, particularly the fine 'A' grade cuts of bacon earmarked for export to England. Many a side of bacon, stamped for the London market, my mother and Michael Sargent renegotiated for their local consumption. The division of a side of bacon was affectionately negotiated in Sargent's drawing-room in the red-brick house in Cook Street. 'Lady Elizabeth,' Mr. Sargent used to plead, 'you've got the better of me yet again.' And my mother would reply, in a simpering tone, 'Ah, Mr. Sargent, you're a true gentleman.' She always parted with the larger cut of bacon, courtesying to Pauline, Mick Sargent's demure and sceptical wife, as she exited their house.

Mick Sargent's cut of Robert Keane's bacon was a pleasure to boil. Mrs. Norah Foley would check that the bacon was a bright pink colour and the fat firm and creamy white before she selected a four or five pound piece of gammon. She placed the meat in a stewing pan with onions and cold water (enough to cover). After the water reached boiling point she simmered it over a moderate heat for twenty-five minutes per pound and then twenty minutes 'for the pot'. In late spring or early summer a Savoy cabbage was cleaned, quartered and the larger leaves chopped; the whole dropped into the simmering stewing pot with the bacon for twenty-five minutes. The cabbage was lifted and drained before the bacon, then dropped into a hot saucepan containing 2 ozs of heated butter. When thoroughly steamed in the buttered saucepan it was placed in the oven to await the bacon. Sliced hot bacon was always served on a bed of Savoy cabbage with grilled breadcrumbs sprinkled over each plate. It was a hearty meal.

March 15th 1946

In Brussels you talk again of the mysterious paintings of Paul Delvaux, only months after I brought you to see our young Huguenot, Louis le Brocquy in Dublin. / Mysterious homage to form, mysterious heaven of an essential world. Architecture of *Femmes devant la mer*, Magritte mystery of *L'entrée de la ville*. / How strange it was to meet again at the Palais des Beaux-Arts, the post-War home of Delvaux. / After war, is the world real or is it a statue? You ask, laughing. / Pay homage to beauty standing still, to Doric columns untouched by bombs, to shadow and maps, to trees still upright and a full paper moon. / I cry luxury, luxury, luxury. Art a luxury in a land where five million children starve each winter. I cannot square the logistics of God's purpose. Nor can you. But coffee and tiny pieces of olive bread in a Belgian café, your laughter that crackles through an officious afternoon. / But you have your official duties, still, and all that reading. / Like today, when you turn to the tasselled lamp of our Belgian hotel to read again the far too complex thought of the Frenchman, Merleau-Ponty. He attacks your

hero, Koestler. He explains kindly the Moscow Trials. / But you lament
the decomposition of our Liberal world, that and the coming death of
children. / We think of Delvaux's statuesque women, sensual yet sexless.
And neutrality. / None of us can stand aside any more, you whisper, in
a tone that I recognize from the war. Rubashov and his Fifth Column,
immorality of Opposition. / Here, an art gallery for the innocent and
the persecuted.

Óstán Claridge's, Deire Fóghmhair, 1946

Sa mbiadhlann i gClaridges cuireann tú tuairisc orm faoin ngrádh.
Bhíos gan focal a rá, chuir mé an saoghal ó chrích orm fhéin.
Laethanta an chogaidh mar ghráfaí ar an mbord againn. An uair san
Ní raibh faic le déunamh againn ach pósadh agus dul i dteannta.
'Cuimhin leat d'fhear céile marbh, an tAimiréal san ua';
An cion tobann eadrainn fhéin, coróin na baintrighe agat –

Glór na biadhlainne: bhí gach neomat beannuighthe le cion
Ach tháinig rothán ort le gach rud do bhí i gcoinnibh ár searc-ghrádha.
Gabhtha i gceo Londain. Bhí tú faoi gheasaibh mo tháimhnéill
An oidhche san. Bhí orainn fanacht sa fhód neódrach –
'Beidh branda, nó dhó againn, a stór.' Do leagan cainnte
Leis an ngrádh a bhí múscailte; leis na h-uaireanta a chuir an ola orainn.

Teidhleacan sa Gheimhreadh, 1944

Coinnle laga na gréine; smólach glanrúnda na nDaicheadaí
I roilig éadóchasach na Feabhra; na Gearaltaigh sa chill so
Ag dreo san uaigh. An chré chrua an namhaid is measa athá romhainn,
M'uncail bocht. Paax agus a dheatháir leithlisteach

A dhein an sclábhaidheacht; a bhean is a mháthair
Mar chomhluadar ar mo mháthair fhéin. Cad a dhéunfaimid
Leis an talamh naimhdeach so? 'Cuimhin liom na ranganna
Cois abhann, machnamh muar sna sean-ráite aige.

Dorchacht an Gheimhridh. Templemaurice an phairc phneimh –
Díospóireacht na scoláirí mar uisge ionlaidh; treabhadh cuaird
In-a shaoghal: Captaen Mac Gearailt, ní bheidh do leithéid aríst ann!
An Déan ó Lios Mór grocaithe leis an bhfuacht, An Seanadóir Keane

Ag guíochant chun Dé: iad go léir mathanóirí
Na neodrachta. Mise an mac leis an Eoraip phráidhneach, ar díth
    cáirde:
Ach is deacair an nuacht d'fháil ón bhfilidheacht.
Is fuath leo an ré nua ar lár, na tíortha nach maireann.

An Gearaltach is uaisle curtha fé'n bhfód i gCeapach Chuinn,
An Geimheadh gan trócaire ag baint taca as na crainn;
Gaoth Shliabh gCua ag cur faitís orm. Mar bharr ar an donas
Thuit an Bíobla as mo lámha, an bhileog cheangail stróicthe;

Reodh seaca ar bhriathar Dé: *Molaidís Ainm an Tighearna:*
A Ghlóir ós cionn na talmhan agus na nemh. M'Uncail
Bocht curtha sa chré gan Pádraig Denn nó an t-Athair Hennebry;
Cailíní an pharóiste ag canadh Na Connerys; Paax ar a bhosca ceoil.

January 8th 1947

In London, again, in transit in a decade of transits, we meet and walk
and make love with the familiarity of the married. / I have poems from
home and the making of poems. We talk of the old Cornerstone town,
of this day and Mrs. Norah Foley's devotion. September 8th and
Cappoquin's Pattern Day, that Feast of the Nativity of the Blessed
Virgin. / How many will walk the Old Road to the edge of Sir John
Keane's garden to do their rounds, to recite their Rosaries? / You want
to hear poetry in a language you can't comprehend, a poem of Raftery, a
poem of Ó Rathaille. And I slip in here a poem of my own making, two
poems of the Normandy battles. This language is like a canvas tent we
throw over ourselves in a café at Charing Cross. / All the while you are
waiting to leave, one eye on the long railway tracks south, the long road
to Europe's sunlit marketplace. / And I quiz you again, half in jest,

pester you, mimicking the insufferable and indiscreet colleague. / Why are we scattering when we should be together? Settle down. / You shrug, annoyed to be pinned down, even in jest. / What are you up to, beloved? / Listen to this, you say, listen to this, poet. A Decree of the Central Committee of the Soviet Communist Party. / Listen, poet: *The magazine* Zvezda *also broadly popularizes the works of the writer, Akhmatova, whose literary and social and political personality has long been familiar to Soviet society. Akhmatova is a typical representative of the empty poetry without ideas which is alien to our people.* / After which she nudged my ersatz coffee cup. / Drink up, beloved, if Boston's bourgeois in-laws don't get me, your European Communists will.

Cappoquin House Liver Cooked in Cream with Herbs and Croutons

Things were looking up for these friends of Paax Foley, these three hard-working labourers known in Cappoquin as Hobbles, The Fitter and The Warrior, on their first week of discharge from the Irish Army. They got a job from Sir John Keane felling timber at the back of Cappoquin House; and the woman of the house, full of the joys of life after her release from the tedium of the Emergency – and pleased that The Fitter or The Warrior collected her *Daily Mail* from the afternoon boat-train each day – served them this delicious dish on a pantry-tray in the potting-shed. Ever after, the three men annoyed Mrs. Norah Foley with tall tales of the fine *cuisine* at Cappoquin House. Yet at Templemaurice itself the process of writing was always associated with baking. There were entire childhoods spent watching Mrs. Norah Foley baking in the huge Templemaurice kitchen while waiting for Uncle Walter to take the household to Irish lessons in the summer-house. If Uncle Walter was really absorbed in his Irish studies he often missed dinner, but ate earlier: a kind of 'hunt tea' of liver, bacon and brown bread.

The way that the rather stand-offish cook of the grand aristocratic Cappoquin House and Mrs. Norah Foley of Templemaurice House cooked their lambs' or calves' livers were one and the same: the liver was sliced into ½-inch cutlets and fried very gently, sometimes with the addition of sage and sometimes floured and salted. Here are the ingredients for the dish that Hobbles, The Fitter and The Warrior enjoyed on that cold afternoon in Cappoquin in 1947:

1 lb of liver
A sprinkle of dried sage
A sprinkle of thyme
1 onion
4 small carrots
1 young celery stalk
3 tablespoons of breadcrumbs
1 cup of sour cream
Half cup of vinegar
Pinch of salt
1 oz of cooking fat

Drop the sliced carrots, celery and onion into the frying fat. Add the thyme and sage to this. Drop the sliced liver, lightly salted, into the stewing vegetables and cook all for ten minutes, stirring occasionally. Then add the breadcrumbs, sour cream and vinegar and continue the cooking until the liver is lightly cooked. If the mixture thickens too quickly, thus preventing the liver from cooking through, add a little vegetable stock. The entire cooking process should not take more than twenty minutes.

Turn out into 2 heated plates or 4 plates for picky eaters.

Mrs. Norah Foley's Helvick Harbour Fish Base

Mrs. Foley always called this concoction 'Helvick Harbour Fish Base' but my mother insisted that it must have begun its West Waterford life as a classic French *bouillabaisse* in the kitchen of some Blackwater Big House. Mrs. Foley sometimes marinated firmer pieces of hake or sole for three hours in a mixture of olive oil or soy sauce, parsley, thyme, saffron and orange peel. The chopped tomato was always optional, but Mrs. Foley never added tomato to any cooked dish without first removing the sour seeds or adding a spoon of white sugar.

½ lb of crumpled pre-cooked crab meat or sliced mussels

1 cup white wine

½ lb of sole in inch pieces

½ lb hake in inch pieces

2 tsp ground saffron

3 tablespoons soy sauce

1 tsp thyme

1 tomato chopped

1 tsp sugar

Bay leaf

3 onions

3 medium-sized carrots sliced

2 garlic cloves

5 tablespoons of butter

2 quarts water

6 slices of toast or reheated/toasted Barron's Bread

If using mussels steam them at first for four or five minutes. Warm the wine and sift the saffron into it to dissolve slowly. Put to one side. Melt butter and then add the onion, carrot, garlic, all seasonings and, finally, soy sauce. Simmer covered for 5 minutes. Then add the warmed wine and water. Bring to boil and then add fish: hake first, then sole. Add the cooked crab-meat, reduce the heat and simmer for a further ten minutes. Remove from heat and serve immediately with warmed or toasted Barron's Bread. Once or twice Mrs. Norah Foley melted shredded Gruyère cheese on toast under a grill before serving with the Fish Base.

This serves 6.

February 13th 1947

On they go, singing in the unforgiving cold of a February day / Two of those red-haired Foley women singing old songs of the tyrant-landlord and the cornered Fenian. Even the Word of God has frostbite in this bleak country *Praise ye the Name of the Lord. His Glory upon the Earth and the Heavens.* Uncle Walter put in the ground, earth that holds

Father Hennebry and Percy Ussher. Waterford earth. / Earth as dark as winter now, Templemaurice that has offered up its crops, great harvest of scholars; a straight furrow ploughed in his life. / Hopeless grave of winter, earth of sourness, hard earth that breaks the spade / Paax Foley and his huge brother doing the spadework, his wife and mother the soul-companions now of my own poor mother. / Captain FitzGerald, the last of the Geraldines in this place, last scholar-Geraldine, his likes never seen again. / The Dean of Lismore is overwhelmed by the winter cold, Sir John Keane in conversation with the undertaker; all the perished survivors of neutrality / Myself out of urgent Europe, unable to bring the news through poems / All who hate the new era upon us / Let Erin dis-remember the disappeared nations. Now, a weak candle of sunlight / the sparrow of courage / all together in this winter of despair. A Bible falls from my hands, grief's torn end-papers. And that sound, everywhere, that sound floating in the despairing Knockmealdown winds. / Paax Foley's melodeon following the women as they go on singing, skirting around the winter mourners. Wind, merciless, sheltering in the trees.

Mrs. Norah Foley's Carrageen Moss Jelly

Mrs. Foley loved her Carrageen Moss Jelly. She sometimes substituted milk for water in the recipe, but Lady FitzGerald preferred the clarity of the water base.

> ½ lb of moss gathered after rain
> Grated lemon rind
> Sugar

Gather the moss after a soft shower of rain. Wash well and put in a saucepan of 1 pint of water with grated lemon rind. Bring to boil and simmer for half an hour. Then add sugar and strain into a glass bowl or wet mould. Turn out onto a dish when cold.

St. Patrick's Day and the bleak shamrock and the bleak German spring.
/ New Guardsmen step and turn to perfection under a barking RSM. /
I feel as desolate as a small country going down the drain. Ireland in the
grip of some terrible lack of ease, squeezing her sons to Dagenham and
Cricklewood. / I carry my tray of shamrock like a Pastoral Letter out of
Waterford and Lismore: food for thought, inedible. / As inedible as the
fish stew of San Remo that seems to taste still in my mouth. A mistake
to go south without her. / We broke away too soon. She broke away.
America calling, NY to Southampton. / What we had was as sudden as
the flowers of Ventimiglia, worn down by the cruel Ligurian heat, left
naked by the mistral. I think of her body then like the narrow cage of a
boy, a blush grape, slender, a waterfall of hair in passion: every move of
this Wellesley woman a kind of haunting; nights of the fragrant south in
bed with us then. / Across Europe of so many single men, the erotic
posters. So many trembling with sex for food. But her perfection
nowhere to be seen: I wait for her on the dry sandbank of loneliness, on
fire with memory, thoughts like dreams among the flower markets. / I
image her nylons on the floor, somewhere in America. Not a word. /
Never to reveal oneself, not soon enough. An early March without her
by the sea. Foolishness. As if to heal myself I fall into conversation with
a waitress, her husband dead in the war. But in San Remo, you are the
one I search for: no stranger drinking her hopeless Asti. / Insistent,
pushing forward, this empty St. Patrick's Day.

Camera Matrimoniale, San Remo, 1948

An grádh Iodálach athá againn chomh tais le h-ológa cumhra:
Tú féin súgrach, ar meisce, tar éis an chithfholcaidh.
'Cad a thaitnigheann leat, mo Choirnéal?'
Thá ligean chuige agus uaidh agat, mo Mheiriceánach –

Tusa ag iompú ar na bráillíní línéadacha i Liguria,
Do mheala-géaga ag cur ceisteanna orm, do thóna coimre

Mar ubhla úra ó ubhall-ghort na h-Eilvéise, buí ón ngrian.
Spréighim ola olóige, ola Tuscánach, ar do chorp dílis.

An t-súmhaireacht dá meascadh againn, mise Titian, an sgriosamhnach,
Is luighe na gréine dá phéinteáil agam i San Remo –
Ach náire orm faoin nglór, glór do mhúnlóireacht corraithe,
Mo scuab sáible reisiminte ag cigilteach do thóna.

May 18th 1948

DELASEM / Sit down, you say, stand still and you will learn some things about this war. Don't believe everything you want to believe because you are a British officer, an Irish poet. / When I moved from Bordeaux to the Haute Savoie it was not a good time. / I carried ink and type to that Doctor of Judaism, Father Marie-Benoît: such a man, in a damp cellar in a monastery of Marseilles. A Capuchin, of course, they are always up to something daft. But hundreds crossed into the Italian zone, and hundreds more to Switzerland and Spain. / How strange it was that we should meet at Camberley as I spoke about the Madonna in the art of the Veneto. Believe me, every girl of the Veneto is beautiful and deserves to be the Mother of God. Your face lit up when I said that. I was sure you were a Catholic, instead of the Church of Ireland agnostic that you are, believer only in the sacredness of psalms and poems. / Where did you learn all those ancient prayers? / Now the Communists here in St. Remo attack Pius XII, but Pius told Lospinoso to keep his mouth shut, and through this the rescue went on. I've seen the estimates / 50,000 souls, but thousands lost. / Blame Europe, Mister Geraldine, don't blame poor Pius. Even the Regime Fascista attacked my Church for obstructing the Final Solution, for that crime against a New Europe. / Beware, dear poet, of this phrase, *The New Europe*. I'm beginning to hear it again. / Diplomats of the Hospice Santa Marta signed 6,000 passports. And my countryman, the Primo Notario, has played a wondrous game. / Ah, such coffee! Such a joy to see Italy rise again. Here is my medallion from the late Cardinal Boetto: *Ne pereant probationes.* / God willing, all who survived will make a Holy Land.

Ceisteana faoi Titian, San Remo, 1948

Na rudaí oiriúnacha ar bharr mo theangan agam,
Ach ní raibh focal uaim. Síodúlacht an ghrádha,
An bheirt againn gan aon rún eadrainn:
Tú marbh leis an gcodhladh, sínte síos go caoin,
An suirí déunta linn. Do cheathrúna
Dá dtaisiú ag an bhfilidheacht is an chuimhne.

Bhíomar ag caint faoi Titian, obair ardéirime
Na hIodáile, siosarnach na Meánmara
Ar an ard-siléail, scuab-phéinteála
Titian ag ullmhughadh seomra cogarnaighe dúinn:
Titian leis an spéirbhean, ciaptha ag an gcíocras

Mar sin fhéin, mo ghrá mílítheach –
Gan fhios ar bhléin, gabhal ná glúin.

Aonach an Déardaoin i gCeapach Chuinn, 1948

Grian an Fhóghmhair ag taitneamh i bhfuinneogaibh siopa Frahers;
Gurnán an chogaidh thart orainn, seana-shaighdiúirí mar bhóithíní Dé
Sa Stoirm; an domhan ag lorg foscaidh faoin bhfeochadán –
Mar a bhfuilim fhéin anois, sa siopa-chlós Dinny Mescall,

Bhí na hainmhithe ag gearán go géar ó mhaidin,
Caoire ó Chnoc Meilirí, beithigh lena nGiúdais shábháilte,
Na ba imníoch fós fé scairteach na mban; na fir
Ag tnúth le coith leadránach an tigh tábhairne.

Torthaí buigéiseacha na nDéise, marbhughadh na péiste faoi bhláth:
Prátaí úra ón Áird Mhór, cairéadaí Garbhánacha.
Tuigim cumas tógála na neodrachta, 'fad sa lá an tuiscint san –
Is treise dúthchas ná oiliúint, Ceapach Chuinn ná an crioslach cogaidh.

Tháinig triail orm sa nGaoluinn, cosnúg an chogaidh
Sa dteanga dúthchais. Indiu, tagann deighilt ar an nádúr.
Nílim sábhailte fós, mé i mbrón casta sa saoghal so,
Ag stracadh fós ar thriosgar agus slacharáil na nDaicheadaí.

August 17th 1948

It is certainly not the *seanchas* of Tomás Ó Mhuirthe, or anything in his
world, said Percy Ussher, nor has it the received spirit of the Gael, or
the learning. But it is not every man's duty to be a scholar: some are
called merely to be witnesses within the language. / And Mrs. Keane's
Unionist cousin from Helen's Bay, a dapper young barrister with an old
Goertz camera, flits in and out among the tables at Walsh's Hotel. He
records with a frantic energy the peculiar, indolent summers of the
South, as if at any moment the Free State might disappear, the entire
projects of the Gael dissipate in a wave of Ulster Reason. How lucky he
will be, this agent of history, to have the album, the evidence. / *Bhuel,
tá aithreachas mo chroidhe orm nár thugas céird an tinncéara dhuit-se* said
the scholar-headmaster F.X. O'Leary who had stopped when offered a
cup of tea in the middle of the afternoon. And Arland Ussher laughs in
recognition: for what is fluency but an openness to receive words from a
ploughman? / We have been arguing about MacLiammóir, most senti-
mental of Irish writers, most colourful, most cockaded. Percy's Gate
friend. It was Mrs. Keane who claimed that she could detect a little of
the 'actor's jealousy' in Percy's dismissal of Michael. Not all of us have
been offered the gift of a ploughman. Laughter / In the summer after-
noon, Ireland like a molten liquid, in a free state, years of re-invention,
words transformed like personal names, land where a man is born not to
his mother but to his *nom-de-guerre*. / And we taste, yet again, that
Cappoquin liver cooked in cream, the small effort at croutons, the taste
of Cappoquin fields. / Think on this, Mrs. Keane said. What does it
mean to be melted down and re-made. / And Ulster's Goertz camera
working quickly, not convinced.

I Lios Mór Mochuda le Mícheál Mac Liammóir, 1948

Deire Fóghmhair cois Abhann Móire, is na Déise ag cur suas
An phúdair. Bhí laethanta ann agus bhí Lios Mór dathúil –
1948. Olltoghchán thart, an lucht nua sa Dáil.
Bhuaileas de Mícheál i gcomhluadar Clodagh Anson agus Bean

Uí Dhoughlas. B'ait an oidhche san sa gCaisleán spad-chluasach.
Mná galánta, coinnle céirbheacha ar an mbord místuama;
Gloine Phort Láirge lán den chláiréad St. Julien.
An comhrá chuireadar i gcóir i dteanna 'chéile

Ní raibh tada le rá againn fé'n gCogadh domhanda,
Ach Mícheál ag cainnt fé'n Gate is Orson Welles.
Duilleoga na mbliadhanta ag druidim anuas, aisteoir fé sholas
Na mban, fionghloine briosg: daoine ionta féin iad san.

October 3rd 1948

I carry a year-old magazine in my satchel / Volume XVI. Number 92. *If
you have liked anything in* Horizon *this year, send the author a food-parcel.
Orange juice, tomato juice, butter, bacon, rice, tea, honey and tinned meats
are all particularly acceptable to brain workers. They take two months to
arrive so you could begin now.* Horizon *undertakes to see that all parcels
addressed to authentic English artists, whether they contribute to* Horizon *or
not, are safely delivered to them.* / And with this London review of art
and literature, you send a parcel to me, your poet friend in the German
darkness of the Armoured Brigade. Then add: wrong language, I agree,
but you're the only poet I know. You and your literary sister have sent
other parcels to people 'who suffer more', like George Reavey's editor at
Lindsay Drummond, Wrey Gardiner's of the The Grey Walls Press and
Storm Jameson's man at Macmillan. / So, those tinned meats from
America, biscuits in light green boxes, tinned Canadian salmon, two
dozen Hershey bars. Each tin seems to say 'Remember me.' Of your
kindness I make a German hoard of gold. / With news from elsewhere
not so good. Whispers of war and uprisings in the East; and from

Palestine, a catalogue of Irish Guards woes, Irishmen falling in love with Irgun terrorists: that eternal Western chess game of espionage. / I think of the wretched at Sandbostel, and the wretched of Europe still wandering. / While we console ourselves with Freud's night-dreams, Freud's polar extremes, banker and communist, cardinal and commissar. / In the midst of this misery, catalogue upon catalogue of the under-nourished and un-housed: we chisel our destinies from a fallen ash tree, resilient, enduring. We carry these unbroken yearnings on the banks of the Elbe, order and esteem, love and honour.

Tallow Fair Lamb and Aubergine

Tallow on the banks of the River Bride was famous for its horse breeding and its horse-fair. It was in the heartland of point-to-point country, a place of muddy and whiskey-soaked afternoons every winter and spring. But Tallow Fair was also noted for its sheep and lamb sales, small bargains struck at the end of the horse-trading. My mother claims to have got this recipe for lamb and aubergine from a Tallow grain-merchant called Harris with whom she seemed to have had a very intimate friendship when she was a farming widow in the early 1920s.

> 1 lb of good neck of lamb
> 1 pint of stock
> Juice of half lemon
> 1 tablespoon of tomato sauce
> 1 large aubergine
> 3 sliced onions
> 3 ounces fat
> (N.B. water can do instead of stock)

Slice onions well and fry in fat until browned. Cut meat into small pieces and fry with onions until browned. Season, then add stock or water, tomato sauce and lemon juice. Dice the aubergine into little cubes, add to pot. Bring to the boil and simmer gently for at least an hour. Serves 4.

Lady Elizabeth FitzGerald's Rhubarb Purée

2 lbs of rhubarb

5 oz sugar

5 tablespoons of water

Cut rhubarb into two-inch lengths. Put the sugar into the water as it begins to heat. When dissolved add rhubarb. Close the lid of the pan and let it boil away until tender, about 25 minutes. When cooled place in a jug in fridge or cooler. It will keep for a week. Serve cold with pieces of finger sponge-cake or Guards Club cake.

November 4th, 1948

Another gale that blows across the great old trees of Lismore, another evening of the post-War years as winter begins to gather in. / Days of remembrance, days of a melancholy wind. / The poor in their poor-house shelter, and the Brothers in their noisy school seek refuge under an umbrella of the Irish language / The native tongue protects us. Limits. Grammar. Such securities as Europe rages on from winter to winter, hunger to hunger. / The streets of our strong towns empty, trains ferry us from Cappagh, Cappoquin, Dungarvan and Lismore of Mochuda. / I motor to Myler MacGrath's old Palace, the house of that book, replenished and burnished by time. / Lismore, indeed, once beautiful. In 1948, in a howling gale, I drive through the long days of its beauty. / Days of a new government, DeValera ousted, Costello at the helm. A new crowd in the Dáil. / There I meet Micheál again, in Clodagh Anson's company, at Mrs. Douglas's castle table. That was a strange evening in the draughty castle. Elegant women, beeswax candles at the indiscreet table; old *Waterford* glasses filled with the best claret of St. Julien. They made an intimate conversation among themselves. Not a word spoken about the World War, but Micheál holding forth about the Gate Theatre and Orson Welles. Outside, in the blue gloom, the fallen leaves of these years flickering down. / Here, an actor glows in the light of two women, their delicate, attentive wine-glasses. / I feel as a leaf blown from very far away, all of Germany blown by accident into

133

this glowing castle room. / Neutrality. Emergency. That gift. A discreet people who keep to themselves.

Lady FitzGerald's Salmon with Spinach Stuffing

This was the last meal that Lady FitzGerald made for her husband when he came home on leave in 1917. He was unhappy with the turmoil of the land, the agitation against conscription and the increasing decline of the Redmondite viewpoint in County Waterford, so she made this, one of his favourite meals, to comfort him and send him on his last journey. Under a perpetual licence that derived from an agreement between the Great Earl of Cork and a Templemaurice Geraldine, and continuously honoured by the Duke of Devonshire, the family was allowed to take thirty-two salmon from the river Blackwater between Cappoquin and Molana Abbey provided that one member of the family produced twenty-four poems in each generation. Even in the worst years, the 32 salmon were always taken; and in the worst of times the twenty-four Geraldine poems of the Déise have been written and presented to the Duke, the true inheritor of the patrimony of Lismore and its rivers and keeper of the Book of MacCarthy Riabhach.

Two 1 lb or 1½ lb fresh salmon fillets
½ teaspoon of strong black pepper
½ teaspoon of salt
Juice of one lemon
3 teaspoons of olive oil

For stuffing use

1 lb mature, coarse spinach
½ lb of mushrooms
4 spring onions, chopped
1 tablespoon of chopped basil leaves
½ tsp of dried basil
1 oz butter
½ tsp of salt and pepper
1 tablespoon olive oil

Place the skinned salmon fillets together and sprinkle with salt, pepper, half teaspoon olive oil, half tablespoon of lemon juice. Sandwich the fillets together and then sprinkle each side of sandwich with salt, pepper, lemon juice and olive oil. Put the salmon into an ovenproof dish and cover. Place in fridge to marinate while making the stuffing. Turn on the oven to very hot (500° F).

To make the stuffing heat butter and olive oil in a hot pan, add the mushrooms and cook for 3 or 4 minutes. Add the basil and pepper and turn down the heat. Then add the spring onions, and then the spinach. Cover and allow to cook for 2 minutes. Then add the fresh basil. Now remove the top fillet from the salmon sandwich and place the stuffing on top. Cover the stuffing with the second salmon fillet. Pour anything left, olive oil, lemon juice, salt, pepper, over the salmon and place in upper part of oven. Roast for thirty minutes.

This will serve 4 guests comfortably, or 6 picky eaters.

Countess of Desmond's Cherry Jam

It was the old Countess of Desmond of Dromana who lived to be 145 years or more, falling to her death after she'd climbed a cherry tree to get at the really ripe fruit. She may have been preparing to make cherry jam, although the Morello cherries at Templemaurice House came from the drastically pruned, fan-trained fruiting stems that grew in the rich, loamy soil of the kitchen garden. The LGO remembers his mother making this jam with Mrs. Foley, the two of them nattering in the kitchen. But he never remembered anyone actually eating it.

> 4 lb of ripe Morello cherries
> 2 lb of really ripe redcurrants
> 4 lb sugar

Put the stalked and almost overripe red currants into jars that are standing in boiling water. Let the water boil rapidly for fifteen minutes. Place the currants on a sieve to dry, having saved the overflowing juices. Add the juices together. Stalk the cherries and put them in a stewpan with 2 tablespoons of water. Simmer until tender. Then place

in a bowl and let cool. Take out the stones, crack open two dozen or so
and heat the kernels. Place the redcurrant juice into a preserving pan
with the sugar and stir until the sugar dissolves. Bring to the boil and
add the cherries plus the juice and boil until set. Add the blanched
kernels when the jam is almost done. Place in warmed jars and cover.

An Ceolann Dearg, 1950

Na Meiriceánaigh ag caint fe órthaisce Bhanc Shasana,
An glór Iodálach as an sean-raidio baicilít;
Mise ag féuchaint ar na sluaighte thíos sa chosán spaisteoireachta,
Mé ag lorg tuairisge mar na Pílears i nDánn Garbhán
Ach níl faic agat dom. Thá clúdach glas ar an trealamh cogaidh,
Níl an oiread fuirsithe againn is athá treabhta acu;
Na mná as Sráid Baker, dóighte 'ge'n tine Naitsíoch,
Thá ár saoirse ceannaighthe thar barr amach acu:

A stór, tuigim anois nach raibh an sgéul iomlán sa nGaoluinn
'Sna laethanta san; tusa ar seachrán san Eoraip dhóite.
Ag cainnt le taidhleoir Gréagach, Na Balcáin i dtreo cogaidh –
Agus an buidéal Seaimpéin athá againn anocht i San Remo:
'Is linn an t-Olltoghchán san Iodáil, ní bheidh
Aon lá eile ag na Cumannaigh.' La aoibhinn aerach spéirghlan
Agus an léirscrios déunta agaibh. An Ceolann Dearg ina dtost.

December 27th 1948

*I can think, for instance, of no traitor so great and so sympathetic as
Alcibiades. There is a kind of clarity about both the vices and virtues of the
ancient Greeks which gives even to their history the form, the outline and the
impressiveness of art.* / You quote the young scholar, Rex Warner, a boy,
you said, a beauty, holding in one hand a dry martini and in the other
that neat and densely printed *Horizon*. / More isolated from us than
Ireland ever was, you say. Not the regular Holyhead ferry, but the long
and sickening ship from Marseilles to Piraeus. But for young Warner it

is all Greece by air: Viking Airlines London–Athens, RAF transport, the Gulf of Corinth, Parnassus and Helicon, the towers of Acrocorinth, Salamis and Aegina. / You read the prose of someone truly in love: go to Greece, smell the herbs and pine. / Outside our drawing-room window the Atlantic torrents flail the trees, penetrate the shrinking Irish casements. / Though it's not Greece that has you fired up, but another country in the sun, your own Italy. You rage again over one of your own, a wayward American. A name I hear for the first time in these days after Christmas, 'Ezra Pound'. / Let it pass, beloved. Was poetry ever meant to save a soul? / *sharp day-to-day observation, erudition, and humorous insight*... You quote a critic with rage, with rage, your martini spills upon the frayed carpet, our fire splutters with a downdraft of rain. / Let it go, beloved. All is not lost, nor can ever be with Europe. / Is it not enough that in unreachable Greece there's an English youth taking notes, translating poems? / Alcibiades, will speak, in his own good time, to Mr. Pound.

Oídhche Ghemhridh i Southampton, 1950

Báisteach an longphuirt is ceó cruadh na nDaicheadaí
Is mo ghrá ag siúl, a cosa ag coinneáil liom –
Mise chomh fiáin le cocól, chomh naimhdeach le téile searbh:
Is í féin tar éis fios a tréithe a thabhairt dom.

Fear céile marbh that lear, cré na cille a' cur glaoich uirthi,
Cuimhne an ghaisce, ár gcion salach chun na farraige.
A deirfiúr ag déunamh freastail ar an uaigh, an t-eastát. Thá sgéul
Na h-Eorpa ag dul i bhfuaire, mo fhocail salainn i gcoinnibh na gaoithe.

Tusa an bhean stuamdha anois, ag glacadh an chúraim. Na sluaighte ag
    dul
Leat ar shlí na h-imirce, an sluagh san timpeall orainn nuair a
    chuireann tú
Amach mé san oidhche gheimhridh. Mo stór, mise an preiceallálaí anso
Lem 'chaint ró-bhearrtha, fé ceothmhrán millteach Southampton.

Before we came to the proper recipe for sole and hake, for fish base, for mysterious Carrageen jelly, it was Mrs. Norah Foley's stolen bicycle, taken from the church-yard at Affane Cross on a perfect May morning, her stolen bicycle and the trauma of it, that set you talking about the films of Italy. You had spent a spring 'retraining' in New York. Training for what, I wondered, for there was nothing you hadn't seen in the long War. / No viciousness of Europe was ever lost to you. Wounded in mind and body, you were the beneficiary of our civilization. / But, Mrs. Norah Foley, her torrent of abuse against the youth of Cappoquin, her fierceness as she pounded the cooked crab for bottling, muttering, cursing. / Now, avoiding *The Red Shoes* that has played for over a year in New York theatres, you talk again and again of *Guaglio, Ladri di biciclette, Open City*. We walk together down the steps to the boathouse. It could be happening in Europe, it could be a Hungarian countryside. I remembered, for you, our long Edwardian summer that lasted in Waterford until the Civil War. / In this post-War era youth, released from bombed-out basement and demolished home, races across a continent like a pack of wolves, locusts, drawn into a new warfare against the old. In *Guaglio*, it is still the priest-redeemer who must recover the wounds of his stolen valise, his possessions retaken from the hands of the starving, the infant, the poor. And the frocked priest of *Open City* who must hide his espionage like our Monsignor Flaherty. And now you report that *Bicycle Thief* has been embraced by the National Board of Review: the best film of 1949. You describe in detail the city, the hope of a steady job. / The pounding of Mrs. Foley's mallet, our cursing victim of a theft. / Our waiting jars. / *Want.* / Europe. / *Plenitude.*

Briseadh Saoire i San Remo, 1950

Shroicheamar ró-luath mar bhláthanna tobanna an Mheithimh,
Caillte le brúidiúlacht na Meánmhara, nochtuighthe leis an Mistral.
'Cuimhin liom do chorp cúng mar bhuachaill óg na hÍodáile;
Do chíocha mar chaora finiúna, másai do-chlaoidhte,
Do ghruaig ar nós eala nuair do rug tú barróg ar mhuinéal orm,

Gach iompar cailín Wellesley chomh dímhorálta, chomh h-ainglí san,
Gur tháinig na h-oidhcheanta sa Deisceart allasach isteach sa leaba linn.

Mise ag féuchaint ar ghnáth-mhnáibh ar na póstaeir anghrách:
A stór, mí mhaireann do leithéid in aon áit san Eoraip.
Mná anso ina gcraiceann gnéasach, eachmairt ghruama.
Tháim ag fanacht leat ar eitir-gainí an uaignis, eire a droma
De ghean orm; na smaointe draíochta, an taidhreamh a thagann
As margadh na mbláth: Ali, do níolón ar urlár na maidine:
Tú imithe go Meiriceá, is gan sgéul ná duan ó shoin uait.

B'fhéidir nár thug mé fhéin chun soluis duit, ach fanaim
Anso, mo chroí im bhéul: is leigheas gach bróin comhrá –
Mé ag cainnt anois le bean freastail san óstán, a fear céile caillte aici.
I San Remo, tusa an bhean á lorg agam, ach tháimid tugtha leis an
        ngrádh:
Ólann sí an Asti éadóchasach, í ag cainnt is ag cainnt's ag baint fóidíní
        chugham.
Mise ar meisce, deamhan a bhfaca tú riamh nios measa mé –
'Cheann fúm fé dhraíocht an Mistral, mé ag cainnt fút leis an stráinséir.

October 4th 1950

I am at Brendan Bracken's in Lord North Street. / Magnanimous, tran-
scendent, conciliatory, not as wild as the young man in a chauffeur-
driven Hispano-Suiza, but still a Briton who never left the Gold
Standard: not now, not in 1931. / Born at the turn of the century in
Dublin, said Randolph Churchill; his father was a Tipperary builder,
said Lord Winster; born at Templemore, Co. Tipperary, said the *Daily
Express*; born at Ardvullen House, Kilmallock, said *The Times*. / It is my
mother's cousin in the Union Corporation, an ex-Cable and Wireless
friend, who makes the introduction. / Embarrassment. To what purpose.
/ How could Eyre and Spottiswoode take a Gaelic poet? To what
purpose, pray? / Once the tall frame, the shock of wild red hair. But
now, decline. I have met few who've carried so openly the strain of War.
/ But it is there in Bracken's tall decline, the memory that would shorten

your breath. / Yet he is still a rock of sense, wanting to help, speaking of Londoners who might publish an Irish poet. Poetry is no South African gold. Nor is it financial news. Nobody will rush to hear its gasping secrets. Each time I rose to go he waved me back. Generous heart. But not a fool for poetry. / I have a fourth drink, even cut a cigar. He insists I take it home. / The cold autumn chill when I emerge. / Paax Foley waiting for news, the engine running. / No book, Paax, our memories of the war must remain obscure. There you are. / But Paax still furious. *You can't give up, Templemaurice has to be put in a book. I said to my mother you'd have a book about our War.* / I have the peace of having made the poem. / But a book is what Paax is waiting for.

Bronntanas an tSamhraidh, 1950

Sos beag sna Daicheadaí dúsmánta, mo Hallie i Londain
Agus an ghrian ag taitneamh, oidhche Shathairn
Na Cincíse: eadartha draíochtúil dúinn fhéin.
Thug tú bronntanas glórmhar an tSamhraidh dom,
The King of Asine leis an bhfile Gréigeach;
Teas na Meánmhara as gach leathanach, gan dán.

Anlann Sailéid, 1950

Bhí an t-anlann sailéid a dhein tú dúinn ró-throm;
Do ghúna beag as Antwerp, an sról corcra, idir an gnéas nimhneach
Agus an sailéad nimhneach. Bhí an ghrian ag taitneamh
Trí fhionnúgaibh deisithe Shráid Ebury. 'Tháim tuirseach,'
Deir tú arís. 'Beidh an sailéad san measctha againn sa leaba chúng.'

Detained, yet again, at the heart of a divided Germany. Late sprinkling of snow, falling upon packed snow. I am asked to meet an Irish diplomat, and strange to meet him as I must represent the interests of a different clan. / He is assembling the story of an Irish chaplaincy to prisoners of war, 1941 to '43. My lover's kind of work, mysterious, hardly meant to feed the living. But we talk of the frantic years since 1945, his fluent Irish a joy to absorb, that deep recognition at once between us. / I tell him of my mother's Dublin work, her Save The German Children Society, her frantic entreaties for an Irish 'Bill of Landing' to satisfy the Allied demands; with a Mr. O'Connor in tow, banging on the Taoiseach's door. / *Every child in Dresden is born to suffering. If we don't save Germany the whole of Europe will become a barbaric wasteland.* His words astonish me, said with such un-neutral venom this day of the Christmas season. / I think of the food that bursts from Ireland's seams, salmon smoked and bacon cured, Carlow sugar and Tipperary honey, cheddar from Mitchelstown, Thompson's cakes out of Cork this very St. Stephen's Day. / What a bountiful mildness it all seems from this disvantage point of the Allied Zone. / The Irish Diplomat hesitates, something on his mind. Not my poem that he has seen in a political magazine, but this incongruity in a poet of the Gael, this British uniform. / We bid farewell and I watch his official car disappear into the spitting snow, that grey camouflage as forgiving as time itself. / And think. / I am without the two women in the world that I love, each at the other end of Europe. / Christ, how could I go back to be the boy I was?

I gCuimhne an Chobry caillte, 1950

Anocht leathnaigheann ceo mí-chreatúil ar Londain dearmadach.
Siúlaim liom fhéin, an domhan ag éirí as an saighdiúireacht,
Ré an Ghallóglaigh thart; an chumarsáid fé rath.

I ndoimhneacht mo chuimhne, an tAthair Kavanagh agus RSM Stack,
Agus Paax Foley, sa Chobry. Chuaigh siad fé bhráca
Na hainnise, an bád á sheasamh acu ar aghaidh na bpiléar.

Oidhche i 1946, solus an árasáin i Sráid Ebury:
Solus a chuireann a chlaon-shúil ar na daoine caillte,
Solus na filidheachta i-n a gcuimhne. Thá salann Ioruach

Ar gach smaoineamh agam. Ar mhair go fóill dem chairde –
Oifigeach sa Ghearmáin fós, na Micks i Dagenham –
Thá beannachtaí na díchuimhne leo. Mí-ádh na filidheachta:

An chuimhne iomlán athá agam mar oidhreacht throm.
Anocht, eascrann an ceol as tigh tábhairne i gceantar Naoimh Póil;
Ana-pháirt agam leo. Ach sa mhuirchath Artach, an Chobry caillte.

St. Patrick's Eve, 1950

The sound of Irishmen singing in a pub off the Strand / *Na Connerys*,
like a cry out of the depths of my childhood, its verse reaches me across
the gathering fog. / In the staring silence I order a waterless Powers. /
Continue / *Mise Éireannach freisin*, I say, *Leann ar aghaid leis an cheoil.*
Laughter then, *do you know this song?* And I begin to sing. A song of the
Gael. / My British uniform. / A whiskey glass at hand. / It is the famine
again, things that bind us, famine and emigration, our dislocated
London being. / My uniform disappears in a nakedness of songs; once
more into the gap of conversations, into that hermetic world of the
Gael. / Discussions then, of Waterford and Dungarvan, of Ferrybank
and Cappoquin. Pebbles cast upon me as they make a sound-map of my
replies, my people, until – is it Mr. Foley of Ferrybank, silent at the bar
– who jumps towards me 'I know you, I know you, you're the *fokine* poet
from Cappoquin!' And he pulls a decade of *Comhair* issues from behind
the counter, searching wildly, wildly, while the bar looks on. 'There!
There!' And his hand goes to my arm in recognition. *Scríobh sé an dán
seo, An Chobry Cailte. Foilsithe anseo. Eistigí!* Another whiskey is
produced for me as Mr. Foley reads my poem to the assembled, silent
countrymen. / And, after that, a man steps forward, can I copy your
poem for a niece in Old Parish? / The throng, the family. / *To a poet of
the Déise*, a drinker says. A cheer, then a song. / And still in my mouth,
behind the whiskey breath, Mrs. O'Connor's recipe that my mother

saved, her Helvick lobster, her ostrich feathers. / Their sound follows
me along the Strand. / Out of the depth of childhood I connect with
everything. / Essence of being. / Childhood, poetry / Ireland, in the
early evening fog.

Gracie O'Connor's Lobster Grand

This was an all-time favourite recipe of Lady FitzGerald. She claims to
have gotten it from Mrs. O'Connor, the glamorous wife of a famed
Cappoquin chicken farmer and general cold-store merchant, Michael
O'Connor, after a morning spent discussing Red Cross business in the
snug at Russell's shop. Mrs. Norah Foley was always quite jealous of
Mrs. O'Connor's elegance and class, so that she rarely cooked this
grand dish. One infamous dinner party did occur when Mrs.
O'Connor herself was invited to dine at Templemaurice with the
novelists Mrs. Bobby Keane and Elizabeth Bowen as well as Sir
Richard Keane and Eddy Sackville-West. 'I'll teach dat woman how to
serve lobster,' Mrs. Foley muttered to Maura and she prepared a dish
of sumptuous grandeur. But she was outdone by the young Mrs.
O'Connor who appeared at the door dressed in the most stunning
diamanté and ostrich feathers. Mrs. Foley sulked as she served. This
recipe is, in fact, only a mild variation on the classic French dish
Lobster Thermidor. Ideally the dish should be prepared from scratch;
that is, with a live lobster. But many people hate plunging a live
creature into a pot of boiling water, so it is not cheating to purchase a
boiled lobster from a reliable fishmonger.

> 1 large lobster, cooked, about 2½ lbs
> 6 ounces or so of thinly sliced button mushrooms
> 2 shallots or 6 fresh spring onions, sliced thinly
> 2 egg yolks, beaten
> 4 tablespoons of grated Parmesan
> 3 tablespoons of butter
> 4 tablespoons of brandy
> 1 tablespoon of flour
> 6 tablespoons of heavy cream

⅓ of a cup of finest Chablis
⅓ of a cup of fish stock
1 teaspoon of Dijon mustard
Salt, pepper and cayenne pepper

Cut the lobster lengthways into two long half-shells. Remove the stomach and any other sacs. Smash the claws to remove the flesh. Remove the meat from the halved body and the tail. Place the chopped-up meat in a shallow dish and drizzle with the brandy, then cover dish. Cook the spring onions or shallots in the butter and then add the mushrooms. Add the flour and a pinch of cayenne pepper then, stirring and cooking all the time, add the fish stock. Keep cooking until the mixture thickens into a sauce. Next add the heavy cream and the Dijon mustard and season further with cayenne, salt and pepper. Now pour a little of the sauce over the beaten eggs and drop this mixture into the pan. Stir in the Chablis and check the dish for flavour, adding cayenne if necessary. If you don't taste the presence of cayenne add more. Next, pre-heat a grill to medium-high. Mix the brandied lobster into the cooking dish and stir. Now, divide the mixture between the two upturned half shells and sprinkle with the Parmesan. Grill until the cheese is browned.

Always serve with a mixed salad and steamed rice. A good dry wine, Chablis, but not a Petit Chablis, or a chilled Champagne, is perfect with this dish.

Paddy Dineen's Shepherd's Pie

This recipe, a sort of symphony of leftovers, was given to Paax Foley by Paddy Dineen, a well-known process server in the parish of Cappoquin. It was said that Paddy got it from a down-at-heel Anglo-Irishman who tried to distract Paddy with food so that he wouldn't be served with a District Court order for repossession or repayment of monies owed. Paax Foley claimed that Paddy was cooking this same dish in a heavy griddle-pot on his fireplace in the Nuns' Houses in Barrack Street, Cappoquin, when he himself was rudely disturbed by two Mercy Convent workmen who began to remove the slates from his roof in an effort to evict him for non-payment of rent. When coming to or going from Templemaurice House, Paax Foley liked to stop in Barrack Street to chat with Paddy Dineen and with another old friend, the mysterious Tom Ferncombe.

2 lb of potatoes
2 lb of cold ham or bacon
1 lb of boneless beef
1 onion
1 tablespoon of flour
1 cup of beef stock
1 tablespoon of tomato ketchup
3 tablespoons or so of butter
Salt and pepper
A dash of Worcester sauce
A lump of cooking fat or dripping

Boil the potatoes and peel them when done, but not overdone. Make sure the ham and other cold meat pieces are clear of fat and rinds. Fry the onion in the cooking fat or dripping, add the flour and then gradually add the beef stock (this can be made simply with an Oxo cube). Bring this mixture to the boil, then simmer for three minutes, stirring all the while and seasoning with the pepper and salt. Add the tomato ketchup and the dash of Worcester sauce. Now add the chopped-up meats and simmer for five further minutes. Next, turn the entire mixture into a pie dish or oven-to-table dish. Top this with the cooked potatoes that have been mashed and sweetened with some added butter. Cook this in a 220° C oven. Serve to those who are hungry or to those with memories of old Cappoquin.

A Restorer of Souls

The summer we met was that summer of the long waiting,
Myself just back from Ireland, from neutral Templemaurice
    House,
British officers in mufti in every cinema in Dublin, my uncle
Walter ablaze with the sensation of a new Aran Islands poet –

Máirtín Ó Díreáin of the bright candles that glowed in welcome.
It was a poetry like nothing else in a war-torn world,
A poetry of townland and family, of personal hope and grief.
It was a biography of poems that might have remained untold

But for his personal memory, his personal way with pain.
Nations fall, cities are consumed by fire, refugees stalk
The whole of Europe, yet life is distilled into an Irish poem.
What is a nation for but to cultivate a nation's private talk?

My wings clipped with the knowledge I could never be
A poet as complete in my being as Ó Díreáin could;
Destined ever to be at the edge of Ireland's loyalty,
At war in a neutral place, no disciple of Kuno Meyer,

No natural-born son of the household of islands:
Destined instead like a Polish officer without a state
To fight a war that might never bring me back to poets I love –
To explain myself at the moment of personal death

As a loyal child of Walter FitzGerald, Templemaurice
Of his Irish-language classes and the film-boat of Irish words:
Fragmented thus was my soul, and ruined in truth
By everything that left me a stranger on Déise roads

And Camberley classrooms both. I taught with a heavy heart
The Brigade's *Standing Orders* and the conduct of war
Until she arrived to lighten me with her talk of art:
Her American accent spread untouchable calm everywhere.

She was a Staff College guest talking about Italian art,
Captain Whalen of the U.S. Forces, a Wellesley girl
Who held a Boston Cooler in her delicate left hand;
All eyes were on her and her gracious forties raven curls.

None of us knew then her strange advisory career,
Her expertise in forgery, her knowledge of Titian
And Canaletto and Guercino, that entire constellation
Of Italy, embalmed again in a still-life of unreason;

And her way with currencies, inks, politics and SOE.
At that moment in that vortex of change and war
We all turned to her steady New England accent
For style and certainty. America was what we waited for

In terrified and war-torn Europe. When she moved
The world seemed as simple as the hours before dinner,
Ireland seemed so very far away; Templemaurice
And its hermetic farm now a lost, unreal atmosphere.

She was a certain, sudden, companion waited for
Over long hours. How I dreaded the company of more
Handsome men until she moved to me mysteriously,
As if I'd been chosen by some Greek goddess of war –

For love and companionship before death, for drink,
Her Boston cocktail of champagne and ginger ale,
Her Wellesley sandwiches, her library in Italian script,
Her expertise in a different kind of war; my war made pale

By the quiet loss and exile that she spoke about:
The wicked, personal, Fascist pain inflicted on friends,
The screams of the private, personal cell, corpses
Hanging from ceilings, heroes she would never see again.

How human and sympathetic, at one with the world,
Every ordinary cinema and cafeteria seemed
As I waited for her, expectant, thrilled, in full uniform
Or I found her waiting for me, languid, cigarette in hand.

How American love became as America flooded in,
Still in love with itself, adoring its own discipline,
Yet individual in every way, even in the way of love,
For love came easily to her, a languid offering of limbs

After cigarettes and wine. Love as a new conversation
Began again, love as part of the great preparation,
Her physical act against Hitler; her hunger for freedom:
Nothing in the long humanity of Ó Díreán's poems

Could have prepared me for the poetry in her life,
For she was poetry as film, the projector bulb pulsing
In the background of everything she did and said
As if Chandler had written the script of everything

That happened when she walked into a lecture hall
Or cinema, or bedroom. She was most beautiful naked,
A restorer of souls in bed, God's best forger
Who touched up my life, everything unfinished I had.

She watched and empathized with her mimetic brain
Everything I said and wrote. She quoted me to myself
As if both our lives depended upon it. I wondered,
Often, if she would ever release the code of herself:

Only once or twice, I think. Once, certainly, after
Too much drink, tired with waiting, she revealed
She was the love-child of an Irish Socialist leader,
Whalen of the Cappoquin Soviet in 1923 –

Spirited to America as a doctor's adopted child,
Now a waspish Wellesley girl, artistic as the servant
From whom she was born. Whalen of Affane,
A family evicted for non-payment of rent.

How familiar the world seemed as she spoke,
Mixing another cocktail of Italian vermouth,
Familiar the townlands and the Boston escape,
The Fenians of good family who helped her out.

The world quite suddenly enclosed us in itself,
Not as mercenaries of other lands, but as distinctive
As Déise phrases, as luminous and real.
She became a Lauren Bacall with Irish instincts

And still remains as just that. I pity the love
That invents no memory of itself, that goes
Unconscious of its romance to a battle briefing;
Pity the love that only wears a scholar's clothes.

Everything we did was already tense with death.
Once she came as far as mufti Ireland with me,
Nervous but thawing with the munificence of peace,
Poetry and music in Templemaurice, August 1943.

She rode a horse and trap through Villierstown,
Visited Uncle Walter's ancestral stones at Old Affane;
Cleaned Dinny Mescall's mackerel, picked summer fruit
Compressed into London jam, watched the dawn

Illuminate the tidal Blackwater, herself afloat
In Uncle Walter's fishing skiff, moisture of night
Still on our lovers' words. War was unreal to us,
A foreign thing that hardly dimmed the Déise light.

June, 1944

June 1944 and the automatic, relentless machine of war:
With *Dánta Grá* and Ó Díreáin's island voice
I endure the burden of Eastleigh Marshalling Area.
Buoyed by the sweet alcohol of poems, I go at 0400 hours

On the *Llangibby Castle*, old battered soul. We whine
Two days away waiting for a full Mick battalion,
Mass in Normandy churches, a brilliant Sunday in June,
Champagne at Bayeux, then two hours to move –

I race to the front line with Brigadier Sammy,
A noisy darkness envelops us, sudden storms
Of summer rain; then Monty at Reinforcement Camp.
Lunch and lunch and lunch, then a Canadian attack:

The whole of the French earth erupts with noise,
Four hundred Lancasters go over, clouds of war over Caen –
Two men shot by snipers, Victor Balfour
And David Wigan come by, still full of London fun;

Mortars and shelling, torrential rain, floods
That defeat both enemy and friend; days of welcome
Rest and mobile baths; the last of Dromana marmalade;
Air raids in an orchard, Billy Hartington

Running in for a kill; many tanks KO'd;
Another day of waiting to move, shell-fire,
Days of rest and waiting to be relieved –
Terror of watching, scare of a counter-attack:

Shelling and mortaring, the counter-attack is held.
Wednesday, reconnaissance; Tuesday, shelling;
Another attack at 9 pm and forty killed –
Our eighty wounded return to where it all began.

We make a bad night drive, then a quiet day.
Fortresses go over in their hundreds, wave
After wave of bombs fall upon the Falaise gap;
A long day of movement, memorial services,

Very hot days asleep in the woods,
Attack, attack, churches and farms in ruins:
A fierce counter-attack of self-propelled guns,
Humphrey killed, a rescue of two hundred Typhoons

And 10th Field Regiment's brilliant barrage
Kept up for us beyond the call of love,
Their shells as welcome as the three-mile trek to rest
After handing the gift of war to the Hampshire blokes –

Only to drive, full throttle, into a *bocage* ambush.
Now the metallic terror of entire wheatfields ablaze;
Losing formation, flash and counter-flash, the thump
Of shells off the cave wall, death in a midday haze,

Myself screaming 'Reverse, driver! Reverse!' My hands
In rage pummelling the loader's head, my face
Already blistered with the heat of battle, diesel and oil-
Fumes and camouflage all mud-caked in a grimace

That has been groomed already for certain death.
I am sure of this. Sure, now, that none of us will get out
Alive, yet hopeful that we may take an enemy tank or gun
With a flash of shells. We know the arithmetic and yet

We advance in a phalanx of pure Household rage,
Intent upon the narrowest view of war, the periscope
That carries the light of battle, frail as glass,
To where my finger and microphone abandon hope

In the spirit of every insanity that was ever dreamed
Of war and battle. Poems beginning in bomb-flash,
The hum I heard above the squadron's traffic
Was a close friend of death, the words were Irish

And of Waterford soil: Father Hennebry's voice, Arland
Ussher's mischievous tones. Tigers hunted beyond
Our armour plate, 88mm guns stalked the Regiment;
Sometimes in a field-glass, ages before its dull sound,

I saw a tank brewed, a catastrophic tower of flame
And body parts go skywards. Death covered us
In its cloak, Guardsmen cursed and sang as we stalled
Or dropped into a ravine. Time in its glass froze;

And there, standing before me in a Normandy hedge,
Was the pure Waterford Glass of family, pure crystal
Of memory, ghost of family, aristocratic migration
Of our souls in armour. Tasting cordite, time stood still

And formed whole poems. Layer after layer peeled
Away, Geraldine century after century, until
Templemaurice, both house and garden, sat down
To join a cradle of shells. *Fire! Fire!* The hard recoil

Jolted our tank and we were caught, hedge-high, exposed;
And then, the split metal of seconds in a battle,
Two rockets strip our Sherman of its tracks, a fire
Begins in the gearbox. I drag Paax Foley – shattered

And furious with humiliation – from his gunner's seat.
We run like madmen, Paax screams *Me arse! Me arse!*
Shrapnel from a manifold skims his buttocks, his
Exposed behind too raw and bloody to place in verse

But the trail of blood from his wounded rear
Forms a red calligraphy on the flattened wheatfield.
We scrambled aboard a fitter's half-track
And dressed Paax Foley's wound. Its engine yields

To our persistent hopes. It moves through smoke
And fire while we haul a PIAT-carrying Grenadier
Aboard and seek, like Captains Hendry or Ellison Woods,
The 10th SS Panzer tank that nobbled Paax's rear –

Now the steady 'crumping' sound of mortar shells,
The killing medallions of Montchamp and Sourdeval;
Spandau and sniper-fire, Compton and Jeffries hit:
Cornfields swept with enfilade fire, a day of hell,

As we come to rest, intact, finding a harbour
In the smoke-screened kingdom of Harvey-Kelly,
But no kill for us that day, no quick revenge.
A day of burial follows, broken rifles of cavalry

Mark the graves, and steel helmets in a cursed place.
So many friends are dead by now, hulks of Shermans
That seized up and yielded their frail young crews.
I bury myself in a slit trench, wait, make amends

With a pen and paper, unfold a copy of *Comhar*
From its sheath of parachute silk, and read my way
Back into a landscape of Waterford's Irish words –
The hum of Déise poetry tells me what I need to say

And what I should remember. *Remember this!*
Never forget! Uncle Walter whispers to me beneath
An officer's green camouflage net: and I reply,
Indelible ink of poetry, words to make war complete.

The Liberation of Brussels

Movement at night and the heat of battle: we move again
Through a choking dust of August. Exhaustion sets in.
Transporters, armoured tracks and men seem to drift along
To certain death; flickering tail-lights keep us going

And the multi-layered chatter on the net, a numbered command
And a counter-order, a halt and then sudden moving on.
I drift from command, almost finding a boyish sleep,
To dream in a cradle of heavy Browning belts of Cappoquin

And the memory of a rested day as far away as childhood;
As unreal and sweet. Somewhere in my terrified brain
The sound of an orchestra, strings, Hoffstetter's *Serenade*,
A choir at Villierstown church: music spills over the insane

Rattle of gunfire and the choking smell of diesel on fire.
All of this somehow mixed in flames, a cemetery
Of memories. Moving ghostly through the ghost of Europe
Our diesel engines hum; barks, gasps and the intercom choir.

And then, the race for Brussels, bravest of all Europe's towns,
Rain spitting from the battered flanges, kit-bags and PCs,
As we advance at a gallop through risen Belgium;
'Lismore', 'Achill', 'Galway' and 'Templemaurice'

Plunging eastward, greedy for a kill. Halting our march,
Briefly, to assist a pocket of the Résistance Blanc,
We happen upon a missile caught in a tangle of trees –
Only Pat Foley's curiosity unveils a Hurricane's jettison-tank

Dripping Guinness from St. James' Gate. Laughter in tanks,
Suspicious smells of a peacetime Saturday night, bathe
Our advance with the mists of home. Ahead of us, liberation,
Two 2nd Battalion lorry-loads of Belgian pink champagne.

How we raced. How we came upon a city still asleep
As the Brigade swung east in a great encircling loop,
Freedom encircling Belgium in the Bois de la Cambre.
Then, sweetest to every soldier's battle dreams, the whoop

Of liberation, the shower of hydrangea blossom and fruit.
Men and women climb upon the trucks, clamber across
Tanks to pour champagne and brandy into turrets. Men so tired
From the ninety-mile night-march, they fall to outstretched
    arms.

We wake in a kingdom of the saved, taking salutes
From every man and woman, welding a second storage cage
For good wine. And then rush towards German soil,
Hungry for blood, stories filling us with uncontrollable rage.

Eastward we scurried in the fading light, through marsh
And heavy woods, knowing well the weight of armour
Assembled like wolf-packs in the sodden borderlands.
We assemble at Overpelt and Neerpelt, the day draws near

To 14.35, two Generals on a factory roof, ten Field
Regiments, eleven squadrons of Typhoons; the grid
Of Belgium and Holland gets lost in a cloud of dust
As we advance. Yet only a two-minute advance is made

Before German anti-tank guns make their stand:
Only the gunner in Sergeant Capewell's tank is quick
Enough to blaze a Browning belt, while Mick O'Cock
Counts nine tanks blazing, himself the tenth. As luck

Would have it, in the way of all the Micks, Sergeant
Cowan knocked out the self-propelled with a Mick
In its sights. Then tanks fired shells of red smoke
To mark the enemy: Typhoons came in a screaming panic

From every angle, screaming at zero height in a blaze
Of noise and rocket fire. I held my microphone
To the air, gave Brigade H.Q. a smoking commentary
Of battle: trucks and planes, tanks and shells, the moan

Of earth and sky. We routed the Hoffman Group that day
And the German 6th Parachute; at five-thirty the bridge
South of Valkenswaard was ours; and we count the lost –
Parkes and Ackers, Delaney and Moore, all men of courage.

And then move on. Leaving war graves behind us,
Perennial Irish blood in the soil of Europe, we roam
Through the pitch-black night, lit only by homes
Ablaze. A Geraldine night. I can feel the poems –

I work on a little lyric egg after Valkenswaard
Before setting off again, getting held up,
The German rearguard holding Nijmegen, both bridge
And town, their snipers like stick insects

Upon grey girders. We race to and fro,
Racing frightened in our scout-cars, my unfinished poem
Now at the quiet and unreal land of rest,
Bullets whirring, the Grenadiers coming in

Like neighbours joining in a February shoot at Affane –
Here game is better armed and well positioned.
It is we who flock like birds. Grenadiers moving,
Heavy shells, girders singing their grey songs of death.

We move through Nijmegen as the world burns,
Settle awhile in one stately Dutch home;
Get strafed and heavily shelled while I discover
William Carlos Williams's *Collected Poems*

And read his delicate phrases of fruit bowls
And Paterson motherhood; all the while
Numbers Four and Two Companies being shelled,
Halted by flooded dykes and the vicious bile

Of 88mms, camouflaged Tigers and sparkling
Spandaus that rake our lines with grief.
Our billet is burned above my reading head
And Carlos Williams comes with me, bathed

In the soot of battle, sweating with trauma,
The way a neat subaltern mother might
Give birth, give life to a shining brass shell
About to explode into birth. I ingest the fright

Of new mothers, God of battles and Dutch towns
Disturbed like children out of a still life.
Bullets whistle as I shelter in the CP,
A tank hit by friendly fire, a burst of flame.

We wait and move, wait and move, too late
To relieve the cut-off Airborne in the flood –
We crowd the château at Osterhaut
As the troops move on, the bridgehead

Now abandoned. We move to AAM
Near Elst, relieving the ING. Shells whine
About us still, withering Spandaus hiss;
The bridge again a victim, raped at night,

Grey corpses in grey uniforms on a wet bridge,
Crimson of the bombs as they take our souls:
A book of poems, a New Directions book printed
Far away, like armour plate keeping me whole.

Snow Falling on Germany

Conferences and conversations carry us through the winter:
Dismissals and appointments, redeployment of our troops,
Rebuttals, luncheons at Divisional H.Q., the frost of things
Filling my head, burying poems in a drift of manila envelopes.

The indigo of official stamps replaces a smell of diesel.
I work in the frantic cockpit of XXX Corps. We orchestrate
The movements of armament, food and men. We send
Fifty thousand homeward-bound to rest and recuperate.

Men and women in every club from Brussels to Antwerp
Sing the praises of Horrocks and Gavin. I trace fourteen truck-
Loads of champagne, two trains of refugees, an OSS cargo
     plane
Of rocket-documents from the Russian zone. With luck

We'll get an early German spring, an army of rested men.
Major Whalen and I meet again in the after-Christmas party
Of liberation, Brussels *en fête*, formality of dress uniforms
And dinners. We share in isolation that love and poetry

Of ourselves, and ourselves only in that isolated sense;
A poetry that comes from uncommunicated private grief
And things seen that will never again be mentioned. Cruelty
And mutilation, gratuitous killings: why bother to retrieve

That catalogue of barbaric deeds? Who benefits
From an orchestration of rage? Who is really consoled
In transit camp and bombed household? We jettison
Every detail. We empty ourselves before growing old

Of every habit of unhappiness. And instead of torture
We wish only to read and cook, to delight in sex.
A prodigious future is already formed in every mind
That drives through Brussels; a less complex

Set of hopes and dreams. Men and women can hardly wait
For peace and all that peace means: a house and farm
Somewhere far away, a family business in Lismore
Or a rose-garden in Co. Down. In other words, out of harm's

Way, away from the huge task of reconstruction
And the crush of people. We dream of life without a crowd;
We dream of Dungarvan Bay crab meat and Tallow lamb
And aubergine, of Mrs. Norah Foley's brown soda bread.

Ali yearns to be exiled with me at the edge of Europe,
To disappear into my hermetic kingdom of the pure Gael.
We make love as a kind of problem-solving, crumbs of
Irish Guards' cake on her skin and the moist tell-tale

Currants crushed beneath us. So intimate and personal
Is the world we make that nothing seems quite real.
Even my mother's handwriting on a censored envelope
Has a foreign atmosphere; and the news she tells

Is somehow less convincing, having nothing to do
With our life in Belgium or with the intimacy of war.
The heart is the great entrepôt, the Antwerp of the soul,
That is blasted open, held firm, absorbing wear and tear

Like any port of Europe. My mother's rhubarb purée
I can taste from the envelope. My beloved smells it too
And it brings a flood of tears. Desperate to get home, I recite
The towns and townlands of Waterford, making them new

In my imagination and far more perfect than the towns
We left in Ireland; towns of fervent school-masters,
Emptying glebe houses and seasonal rounds of holy wells.
We both dream of afternoons of love on the Blackwater

And the unaltered still-life of neutrality, the absolute
Diamond of its nature, the hardness of its resolve.
Cappoquin of Padraig Denn, F. X. O'Leary's town;
The Thursday cattle fair during our last summer leave:

Everything floods to the pillow of our imaginings
As I dine at the Brussel's Eye Club or we dance
Together to a flood of American music, that flood of hope
That spills across Europe. Ali Whalen loved the chance

To show her paces, to create uproar with her style
And forcefulness, to be watched and loved and dreamt of
By the very young in uniform. The citrus fruit
Of intense days, American sunlight from those groves

Of Eastern colleges and New York schools, all intensified
Into a burst of glamour at Divisional H.Q. Intense
Was that poetry of peace, that flirtatious hum
Beneath everything. Reading letters, I tried to make sense

Of the small annoyances my mother spoke of: the lack
Of stationery at Villierstown P.O., the shortage of turf
On the Dungarvan train, Mrs. Foley's stolen bicycle.
Here, dance and devastation, the sublime and the rough

Days of liberation, starvation and champagne, all
Tumbled together into an improvised and highly mobile
Life. I add two lines, or three lines, or maybe four,
To a modest Irish poem. I think of Irish scholars in exile

In the old days, making complete and arrogant sense
With their trenchant Latin. Snow falls on the Irish words
I use to capture the moment. Bleak is the drift of snow
Eastwards. Champagne of victory falls on others as snow.

Snow falling on Germany, snow falling this early November;
I move through a whitened Europe in Goering's train.
Bleak and grey, bleak the defeated world seems, bleaker still
The snowy winter prospect. Crushed cities and defeated men

Appear and dissolve across the blast-proof carriage window.
I feel un-Irish now and Imperial in a victor's uniform.
How far away Ireland seems on these rails to Dortmund,
Smooth in its Celtic distance, the undamaged gold of home.

Baden, Württemberg and Hesse are broken into foreign zones,
Saxony broken, as full of holes as the Frankfurt-Wiesbaden road,
And Cologne in ashes; Cologne where Dr. Ratzinger met me,
Surprised and humiliated, bookless and waiting for food:

How shocked he was to see the child of a scholarly Irish house
In a British uniform. 'Do you not have your own army?
Do you not have honour of your own?' I could not argue
With a defeated friend of my uncle, but I let him see

The eight poems I'd manufactured out of the heat of battle.
He laughed at my incompetence, but I had the food
Rations and the wherewithal to give his children comfort:
Food as sweet as Sir John's pudding, as Mrs. Foley's bread –

They stare in amazement at an Allied officer who seemed
To bring honour to their embittered father. I gave to them
American chocolates and a bog-oak piglet from home –
A mascot from a neutral place, a land of future welcome.

It was that object more than any ration or promise of help
That filled their eyes with tears; a gift for the three sons
Of a tyro-Fascist, a gift that breathed of a neutral land.
Snow falls on his Celtic past and on their German innocence.

Days of San Remo

At San Remo, knowing how much she knew of this hallowed
Place of pleasure, I sat and waited while she spoke to friends.
The sea and its Ligurian story, laughter on the long promenade,
Wine and flowers, even the crowded casino, might make amends

For the long grief of a Fascist war. Not knowing the heartbreak
That she shared with strangers, friends who never came home,
The Committee to Help Emigrant Jews, Capuchin fathers
And tortured mayors, I could never assess the depth of her wounds.

But she would spring to life after a hushed conversation,
Introduce me to friends of Boston Italian families, to families
And faces once hunted by the Gestapo along this coast,
From Marseilles to Nice, Ventimiglia to Portofino. Now peace

Brings her the full and rounded stories, the close of her
Secret war has to be personal along these sunlit villages –
The full story and destiny of each father and lover lost
Would never be unburdened to me, none of her images

Would be painted upon our times together at San Remo:
It was love stuff with us, the simple stuff that's in novels,
Warmth and lust and poems far away from London;
Her fingers on a wine glass or Bowen's *The Heat of the Day*,

While I tried to make the most of *Christ Stopped at Eboli*,
Dense and socialist memory for the days now growing dark.
Levi's prose reminded me of something in Ó Díreáin's world,
Rocky and elemental; a book like O'Flaherty's basking shark.

How strange books seem in this Europe of abandoned trains;
How humane and immediate: convoys and transports,
The fog of four winters that clings to every station,
Europe's crumbling homes, nothing to illuminate abandoned
    hope.

In squalor the exiled must still dream of returning home,
Twisted rails and temporary bridges, marshalling yards
Covered with canvas awnings; the smell of Europe
Is upon us both, the stench of decades comes southward.

Each train was a travelling country, *patria* of occupied wheels,
Each name engraved upon the exile's broken heart:
Here 'Dachau-Berlin-Praha-Bucureşti,' Romanian refugees,
And a train bound for nowhere, the defeated of the Wehrmacht

Standing ten hours in a siding, alone in their own country.
A Polish train remembered, 'Prosze, prosze, aspirin,' ease;
Or an abandoned wagon with a mother milking a cow, children
With blond hair, and a hospital train out of Bern, its wheels

Screaming with impatience, human misery without meaning
Stares in longing with its child's eye. Doctors and medication
Swoop upon a child with an abscessed heel, abscessed
From walking barefoot on rusted rails from station to station.

The Red Cross, the blessings of a skilled diplomat,
The saving grace of indigo stamps, all part of memory
As we walk the San Remo streets, chat and kiss, kiss and
Smoke, flying our own flags like passenger ships at sea.

Here in the locality of olives, blessed place of flowers,
We come to terms. *Cristo si e fermato a Eboli*
Is our book of the moment. You talk of the mountains
And your hero, Gino Bartali, his famous victory

Of this summer, his Giros, his Tours of Lombardy,
And the Campagnola shifting system with its lustful frames.
What he lost in prayers he gained in technologies,
You explain: a secret Resistance messenger crowned with fame.

And you quote Seán Lemass to me, such unexpected words,
Lemass at the Paris Conference of last year:
'Of our own free decision and in our own interests, we have
Come,' – our small land so far away making it clear

That we side with Europe, but with Secretary Marshall's
Dollar bills. So that the trains that shunt and disappear
Into the tunnels and forests of a lost war are like a mirage
As I kiss you. Our century is compressed into a single year.

You are a mystery. That is part of your skill and education:
Posters that speak of deportees and patriots
Line your suitcase still, meetings with Bartali, silent greetings
And an exchange of papers in the dawn flower market,

All seem part of a residue, the settling ash of unseen battles.
My War Office work is paler by far, but has given me time
To think of Templemaurice and its hinterland of poets,
Cappoquin and Tooraneena and Ireland's slow decline

Into a lesser version of Irish life. Heaps of rubble and ironwork,
Trains that catch fire, the shattered refugees of Europe,
All seem somehow to have a more urgent meaning;
And Seán Lemass pleading for Europe's grief, Europe's hope,

Seems apt and welcome and only a catching-up with poets.
That is our opinion, drunkenly expressed. Wine has gone
To our heads, the way Cappoquin bacon and 'large bottles' do.
Europe heals in the warm night air, making drunkenness a home.

We talked our way through books, an intermittent affair
Of alert opinions, walking by the train station or Casino,
Along the Corso Imperatrice, until we reached the secrecy
Of a suite facing the sea. I never got to what you know

On those luxuriant afternoons or dinner-times, for you,
Major Whalen, beautiful in a borrowed black evening gown,
Kept many untranslated secrets. Inscrutable as *trenette al pesto*,
Blended in like a fish, you kept all the Christian secrets of town

In a hinterland and a Europe turning Communist day by day.
You seemed to read all the Riviera di Ponente, from Ventimiglia
To Savona in the once-occupied east, like a familiar text:
Here and there was familiar grammar, further on less familiar,

But all of it, all the time, peopled with the text of people:
Silent some days, but lambent with homes full of heroes.
Old women who had carried equipment from the seashore,
Radios and forgers' blocks, returning with Jewish refugees

Or disorientated airmen or unhappy creatures from SOE
Who had lost their nerve further east, or drunk too much,
Or gambled badly with Resistance lives. Often both sides,
You said, had put a price on a head. You kept in touch

With every kind of life. Buttered radishes and steamed turbot
Made way so quickly for olive smeared on a chunk of bread
Or a burned-black tin of roasting coffee, roadside conversations,
Your rapid-fire response to the rapid-fire of what was said:

So that when you turned for me to loosen the black gown
It was often the burned whiff of a roadside coffee mug
That came off your arm. The urgent response to my kiss
Hid more desperate images. Sex like that was your refuge

More than it ever needed to be for me. For it was poems
I saw placed in every bead of sweat we made together;
The fabulous fleshliness of poetry, lust beyond Ó Díreáin,
Lust beyond Ireland we had, in this hot Ligurian weather.

Abbreviations

AAM	Allied mil...
AB 64	Army ...
ADC	Aide-de...
ARP	Air Raid W...
CO	Commanding ...
CP	Command Post
DELASEM	Delegazione per l'Assi...
	Italian committee to help ...
ER	Emergency Room
ESB	Electricity Supply Board (Ireland)
GAA	Gaelic Athletic Association, an Irish ...
	organisation
HAMB	Allied military formation or battle area
HMSO	Her Majesty's Stationery Office
IMMA	Irish Museum of Modern Art (Dublin)
ING	Allied military formation or battle area
NCO	Non-Commissioned Officer
NSU	NSU Motorenwerke AG, German motorcycle manufacturer
OGPU	Soviet 'State Political Department', i.e. political police
OSS	Office of Strategic Studies, a US intelligence organization
PC	Personnel Carrier
PIAT	Projector, Infantry Anti-Tank weapon
RIA	Royal Irish Academy (Dublin)
RSM	Regimental Sergeant Major
SOE	Special Operations Executive, British secret arm in occupied Europe
SS	Schutzstaffel, Nazi paramilitary units

By Thomas McCarthy

Merchant Prince

In *Merchant Prince* Thomas McCarthy presents two groups of poems, set largely in Cork, and a novella set in Italy, in the period from 1769 and 1831. They tell the story of Nathaniel Murphy: his training for the priesthood, the loss of his virginity and vocation, his flight from Italy, and later his happy marriage and successful career as a Cork merchant.

Poems and prose combine in a poetic fiction which is, among other things, a meditation on the craft of verse and the artistic calling, and a restoration project on a kind of Irishness overwritten by later history.

'There is always in his work a moral overtone, a savouring of certain moments, when he finds a sweet parable for how the world should be, moments of private love and grief that make up a whole universe.' – COLM TÓIBÍN

Mr Dineen's Careful Parade

NEW AND SELECTED POEMS

Memory, love, history and ideas: Thomas McCarthy has a uniquely direct and engaged approach both to the private and the public, which are inseparable in his poetry. His special blend of wit and lyricism is shown to the full in this selection which draws on his five previous books and adds a large group of new poems.

'McCarthy is writing out of a sense of history and community and memory... Although deeply rooted in his own history, he roams widely: he can be both personal and political in different poems in impressive ways.' – TERRY EAGLETON

'McCarthy has a tone which is very much his own, a kind of burnished commonplace. He writes true satires of circumstance.'
                                    – PETER PORTER, THE OBSERVER